Contents

Acknowledgements   v

Introduction   iv

1   Language and communication   1

2   Theories of language development   18

3   The development of language and communication   36

4   Listening and speaking   56

5   The development of reading   74

6   The development of writing   101

7   Bilingualism   125

8   The child who is deaf   146

9   Language and communication problems   159

Glossary   177

Resources   182

Index   185

Acknowledgements

We wish to thank our colleagues at City and Islington College, North London for their support and encouragement. We also wish to thank:

Cynthia Isaac of City and Islington College; Sue Mitchell of Hargrave Park Primary School, North London; Helen O'Grady and Breeda O'Driscoll in Cork and Mary Hallay Witte in Germany for helpful and encouraging comments on individual chapters.

Thanks also to Carmel Ui Airt of the Gaelscoil, Clonakilty, Co. Cork for information on the Gaelscoileanna, and thanks to the children, nursery staff, family members and friends who allowed themselves to be photographed or gave samples of children's writing: Shirley Booth, her daughter Liz, grandson Samuel and granddaughter Emily; Sarah and Alexander Filhol; Jordan Gayle; Emma Loizou and Millicent Matthews; Ann McLoughlin and the Nursery at City and Islington College; Verona Turnbull and St Augustine's Pre-school; Pippa, Rosie and Bridget Monies; Helen O'Grady and Siobhan O'Driscoll. Finally thanks to the editorial staff at Stanley Thornes and to Jill Frankel and Christine Hobart.

The authors and publishers would also like to acknowledge University College London for permission to reproduce the illustration of Abbé de l'Epée. Every effort has been made to contact copyright holders and we apologise if any have been overlooked.

Dedicated to all the members of our families.

Language and communication

PREVIEW

The key topics covered in this chapter are:

- What is language?
- Communication
- Body language
- Communication through art, music and drama.

Language and communication skills are essential for the effective survival of human beings. When we are talking about children developing language and communication, the words 'language' and 'communication' are often used interchangeably. A dictionary definition (**Oxford English Reference Dictionary**, 2nd edition, 1996) considers language to be 'the method of human communication, either spoken or written, consisting of the use of words in an agreed way'. The same dictionary considers communication to be 'the science and practice of transmitting information'. Communication is therefore the exchange of ideas and information between two or more people. Speech, both oral and written, is the usual method of communication, but human beings can also communicate through a variety of other mediums – for example, through manual communication, music, art and drama.

As children learn to use language, they also learn the appropriate times to use it within the context of a social situation. Very quickly – by their fifth year in most cultures – they are expected to be on the way to becoming literate human beings and to understand the use of written symbols to convey ideas and information. Many children will be exposed

THINK ABOUT IT

Imagine a situation where you had no vocabulary to describe a situation you had just seen and wanted to communicate to others. In addition you were unable to use spoken language. How might you communicate?

to more than one language, even from birth, and most children will be expected to learn a second or third language, either when they enter school or later in their school career. A smaller, yet significant, number of children will experience a range of difficulties when learning language because of disabilities, either inherited or acquired in their early years. Adults looking after young children need to have an understanding of how children acquire language. They also need to have some understanding of how cultural and social factors influence this acquisition and how children can best be helped to become competent language users and communicators.

WHAT IS LANGUAGE?

While thinking about communication in the exercise above, you probably realised how very dependent we are on the spoken language we possess. But what is language, and where did it originate?

DEFINITION

linguist someone who studies the way language began and developed during the course of human history; also studies the structure of language

The origin of language

Despite the fact that language has been studied by **linguists** throughout history, we know very little about its origin. People must have speculated about how language first originated from the time they first began to reflect on themselves. Investigations by linguists throughout history were mostly philosophical discussions and there are records of these investigations dating back to 1600 BC in Mesopotamia. The earliest records of written language date back to 4,000 BC. In the nineteenth century, discussions about language origin were banned because the interest was then on hard evidence and none could be provided to explain the origin of language.

People with religious beliefs believed that language was a gift from God. Judeo-Christian beliefs centred around the fact that in Genesis (the first book of the Christian Bible) God gave Adam the power to name all things. Hindus attributed the gift of language to a female god – Sarasvati – who was the wife of Brahma, the creator of the universe.

Closely related to this divine origin of language is a belief in the special powers or magical properties of language. There were special words to ward off evil or to bring good fortune. In many religions special languages were used for prayers and ceremonies. The first linguist known to us is Panini, who in the fourth century BC considered the rules in the earlier pronunciation of Sanskrit (an ancient Indian language). He is thought to have done this at that time because Hindu priests believed they had to use the original pronunciation of their language for their prayers to be powerful.

Since that time we have learned a great deal about language. We have learned that all languages change through time and that they are all complex and capable of expressing any idea that human beings wish to communicate. We also know that children born anywhere in the world are

Introduction

This book is about how children develop language, communication and literacy skills. Children learn language by being part of a social group which enables them to hear and see how language is used. In a social group they get opportunities for practising and experimenting with their developing skills. The role of adults who care for young children is crucial, as children need feedback and encouragement if they are to become skilled speakers, communicators, readers and writers.

The book is written for students on child-care courses, who need to look at children's language and literacy in more detail than general texts can provide. The text combines an exploration of theoretical issues that students on higher level courses such as the ADCE, HND, Early Years and teaching degrees will find useful. It contains practical suggestions that all child-care students, including those studying for NVQs, the Certificate in Childcare and Education, the Diploma in Childcare and Education and BTEC Diploma in Early Years will find invaluable. Students of other disciplines such as Health Visiting, Speech Therapy and Social Work may also find the text useful as an introduction to the subject area. The book will also be a valuable resource for child-care practitioners who are involved in supporting young children as they learn to talk and take the first steps towards language and literacy.

Activities suggested throughout the book are designed to stimulate thought and discussion as well as to consolidate the reader's learning. Some activities are based in the workplace, whilst others involve groups of students working together. Each chapter contains case studies that translate theoretical ideas into practical situations, and sections that clearly explain good practice.

ABOUT THE AUTHORS

Penny Mukherji, SRN, B.Sc. (Psychology), Cert. Ed (FE), M.Sc. (Health Psychology), is currently teaching at City and Islington College in London. She has many years' experience of teaching on Child and Social Care courses from Foundation to Higher Education level.

Teresa O'Dea, NNEB, ADCE, Cert. Ed. (FE), BA (Psychology), MA (Early Years), is currently a CACHE External Verifier. She has considerable experience working with children who are deaf. For many years Teresa taught on CACHE courses, including the Diploma and the Advanced Diploma in Childcare and Education, at City and Islington College in London. She is a member of the British Psychological Society.

capable of learning any language to which they are exposed. The complex nature of language is still being studied by linguists. It is important to consider exactly what language is before we can begin to understand how children acquire it.

Defining language

Language is essential for human beings for communicating, for organising ideas and, indeed, for survival. Yet it is difficult to define in a satisfactory way. Most linguists and psycholinguists (linguists who study the mental processes used in language and how language is learned) do agree that it is a rule-governed system of **symbols** devised by humans, when they had evolved to a certain level, to enable them to communicate. Making one thing stand for another is a symbol. Sounds, **words**, facial expressions, body movements and letters are all symbols. Animals use symbols too – sounds to warn of danger or the whereabouts of a food supply and dances to attract mates. Much work has been done in the twentieth century on the use of symbolic systems by animals. One famous example is the chimpanzee Washoe who was taught American Sign Language (see page 155) and had a vocabulary of more than a hundred words. At the present time, it is claimed that a 15-year-old pygmy chimpanzee who has been reared at the Language Research Centre at Georgia University has a vocabulary of 3,000 words using a computer which translates keyboard symbols into spoken words. So far, it seems, however, that animals can only go so far, and that they cannot, at the present time, use symbols with the rich complexity that humans can – to recall events, to reflect on a range of subjects, including language and communication, and to share meanings.

DEFINITIONS

symbol anything that represents, or indicates, something else, for instance a doll that represents a baby, a letter representing a sound, a number that represents a quantity

word a sound that is used as a symbol in a language community to refer to something specific

Animals can be taught to communicate

DO THIS!

Make a list of the many ways we use language in the course of a typical day. If you are doing this in a group, compare your list with those of others.

DEFINITIONS

idiom an expression whose meaning cannot be worked out from its separate parts, for example, 'I have washed my hands of the matter', meaning I have no intention of having anything more to do with the matter

phonology the study of the sound units of a language and their relationship to each other

phonemes the basic sounds of any human language. Different languages are composed of different numbers and combinations of phonemes

syntax grammar – the way that words go together (word order) to form meaningful phrases and sentences

intonation the patterns or tunes of speech produced by lowering and raising the voice when speaking

accent the way that words are pronounced in a particular region or country

pitch how high or low speech sounds are, relative to each other, as perceived by the listener

semantics meanings of language

As you complete the task on the left, you will realise how much the use of language and communication is an integral part of everyday existence. We are able to use language efficiently because it is a rule-governed system. The rules governing language make it possible for us to:

- arrange words in sentences so that they have precise meaning
- use grammar to deal with conditions attached to time, for example, 'I was' and 'I am'
- make use of markers, such as full stops and pauses, to enhance meaning and facilitate communication.

The rule-governed nature of language is only a guide and the rules of language can be broken by anyone. There are also exceptions to rules which are in themselves rules. For example, we are all familiar with the rule of adding 's' to the end of words to form plurals. However, in some words in the English language, such as 'sheep' and 'goose', we do not add 's', and so 'sheep' remains 'sheep' and 'goose' becomes 'geese' in the plural form. We also break rules to create nonsense, with sayings like 'Walls have ears', which means you can be overheard even when you think no one is listening, and we use fixed phrases (**idioms**). Language includes the following features:

- **phonology** – the sounds that make up spoken language or signs that make sign language. There are 45 basic sounds in the English language and these are called **phonemes**. Phonemes must be arranged into larger units called morphemes which are words or components of words that have meaning
- **syntax** – the way words are arranged (word order) to form meaningful phrases and sentences
- vocabulary – the words used to communicate
- **intonation** – modulation of the voice – **accent**
- inflection – changing the **pitch** of the voice
- articulation – the act of speaking in a way that can be understood
- **semantics** – meanings of language
- pitch – some sounds or groups of sounds in speech are relatively higher or lower than others.

✔ PROGRESS CHECK

1 What are the usual methods of human communication?
2 Give four examples of symbols we use.
3 Language is a rule-governed system. Give one example of how this can help us when we use speech.
4 Explain the meaning of 'syntax'.

COMMUNICATION

As you have already read, communication is the transmission of information from one human being (or group of human beings) to another, usually using speech, both oral and written. Animals communicate also, but in a species-specific way – bees dance, crabs wave claws, some animals change colour and most make use of sounds. Human beings use sound – speech – but also a rich variety of other methods are used to transmit information, images, thoughts, ideas and feelings. When these are received, they are processed by our brains and stored. They may be understood or not understood, and their content may be rejected, remembered or forgotten. It is important to think clearly about human communication. All aspects of this human skill need to be appreciated, and when working with young children we need to take delight in and appreciate their growing ability to communicate, regardless of the medium used.

Being a successful communicator using any medium is a valuable human talent. According to the philosophy expressed in the religions and myths of the world, this ability to communicate in a rich and complex way is what makes us human and is our source of power. All communicative acts are precious and we need to teach the children in our care to value them.

The list you made for the activity above probably includes gesture, eye contact, body position, touch, sign language, Braille, signals, written language, art, literature, dance. You probably also included e-mail, the Internet, and many more. Each one is a complex system to be used at different times to communicate something, depending on need and appropriateness and on what we have been conditioned to do in certain situations. Communication by any means is not possible without shared meaning and **intuitive understanding**.

Shared meaning

We cannot communicate unless the meaning of what we communicate is understood by those receiving it. This is dependent on the shared meaning

DO THIS!

Spend some time, either on your own or working in a group, listing all the different ways that human beings communicate other than by using speech.

DEFINITION

intuitive understanding
having a feeling or sense that things are a certain way without being told

Shared meaning allows us to understand and enjoy a joke

of the words, gestures or symbols used as well as their content. A child learns very early in her first year of life that gesture has a meaning as well as words. Waving 'bye bye' is an example of this. Nowadays, ways of communicating technologically are globally understood.

Intuitive understanding

This is usually dependant on the context in which the communication takes place and can apply to written as well as spoken or signed communication. 'Let's meet in the pub after college' can have any number of meanings that are not conveyed by the words used. It can mean 'I haven't seen you for some time, so let's catch up on the news', 'I would like to spend time with you' or 'We need to talk about what is happening right now and meeting in the pub is the best way to manage it'. Intuitive understanding can be hit or miss, even when we know people really well, and adults have varying skills in this area. Young children's communication may be far more difficult to understand because they haven't yet learned enough vocabulary and their understanding of the social nuances (subtle differences in meaning) that go with communication may not be well developed. Thus 'I don't want milk' at snack time might mean 'I want to be given some individual attention and this is the only way I can think of saying it'. It is important to get to know children really well through careful observation. We cannot assume that what they say will communicate what they really feel or want.

Communication is also dependent on the appropriate use of:

- **non-verbal communication**, using eyes, hands, facial expressions and positioning of the body, also known as body language (see page 8)
- listening skills
- turn-taking skills
- ways of using language to deceive, prevaricate, fantasise, make jokes, etc.

Communication and young children

Social psychologists who have studied the way children develop into social and knowledgeable beings feel strongly that this is only possible in an environment where adults communicate their language and culture, with all its subtle meanings, to children. Vygotsky called the signs and symbols that we use to communicate 'cultural tools', that is, tools, or symbolic systems (such as language and music) which are used to transmit information about culture from one generation to the next. Vygotsky concerned himself mainly with spoken language and literature, but we are now more aware that any means used to communicate information is valuable if information is communicated effectively. Unless a child is disabled in a way that makes speech impossible, spoken language accompanied by gesture and other non-verbal communication is the primary means of communication. We need also to value and use all the other means of communicating – painting and drawing, drama, stories and myths, both oral and written, and many more. Any communication must be age-appropriate and meet the needs of the individual child. We can only use these means effectively if we value them ourselves as rich means of communication.

DEFINITION

non-verbal communication
any action or gesture or use of the body which communicates information without making use of speech; also referred to as body language

---

DO THIS!

a) Visit a local art gallery on your own and select a picture which you would like to show to a small group of children aged about 4. Make sure to select a picture that you really like yourself. If you do not know already, find out about this picture and some interesting details about the artist.

b) Take the group to the art gallery. Give the children plenty of time to look at and discuss the picture, but do not overwhelm them with information. Then let them see some of the building and generally enjoy the outing.

c) Later that day or the next day, get the children to talk about the picture. Note any information, insight, feelings, or anything else which was communicated to the children via this work of art.

GOOD PRACTICE

- The information to be communicated and the medium of communication used must be age-appropriate – the whole point of any communication is being able to share meanings.
- All communication relies on our ability to use symbols. Give very young children plenty of opportunities to engage in symbolic play, for example, doll play.
- Communication is enhanced if it is allowed to happen in a relaxed non-pressurised way.
- Accept any communicative response, especially if the children are still at the stage of developing confidence in communicating with adults.
- Make children aware of other communication systems, such as semaphore and morse code.
- Children need to be listened to as adults would wish to be listened to. This develops their confidence in communicating.
- Make use of stories, poems and songs. Encourage children to reflect on what a story or poem has communicated –

happiness? sadness? appropriate ways of behaving?
- Play a piece of **programme music**, such as 'Carnival of the Animals' having first told the children the story that it is conveying. Discuss with them how the music portrays certain happenings.
- Encourage the use of mime.
- Where appropriate, encourage children to explain what their drawings or paintings are about. Do this carefully because a child might be upset to think that you can't automatically see what has been drawn/painted.
- Introduce children to the language used by people who are deaf.
- Talk about how people who are physically unable to produce speech might communicate electronically.
- Be aware that your attitudes and behaviour are being absorbed by the children in your care. If you do not want children to do something, do not do it yourself.

DEFINITION

programme music music which is set to a story – sounds and instruments are used to depict features of the story

Encourage children to discuss their art work

We need also to be aware of how much is communicated to children via adult behaviour. All adults are role models to children but those close to young children – parent/carers, babysitters, teachers and child-care practitioners – are particularly powerful role models. In addition to words, actions communicate feelings about people and children, stereotypical attitudes, gender bias, positive and negative cultural views and a very large amount of other information.

CASE STUDY

Jamie

Jamie, aged 3, entered nursery school with delayed communication skills. He had a basic vocabulary but would not usually use the words that he knew and he would avoid communication where possible. He was already attending speech therapy. His parents were very worried about him and put a lot of pressure on him to speak. At a staff team meeting it was decided that Jamie would be given as much freedom as possible to take part in nursery activities without pressure to communicate. Staff would continue to communicate with him in a very natural way, but would not put pressure on him to reply. Even the slightest communication effort, for example a facial expression, would be accepted and if appropriate responded to. Jamie soon began to join in all nursery activities but spent much of his time painting and drawing using all the resources that were available. He would bring his work to staff members to look at and they would talk about it and allow him space to communicate using gesture or words if he wished. Jamie gradually began to talk more, particularly in situations where he was not under pressure to speak, and by the end of his first year he was happily able to communicate with both children and adults.

1 How did the staff team's decision to give Jamie as much freedom as possible help him?

2 How was Jamie helped by their decision to accept any form of communication?

✔ PROGRESS CHECK

1 What is communication?
2 What is necessary for effective communication?
3 What did Vygotsky call the signs and symbols we use – sounds, words, etc?
4 Why is it important for children to feel that adults will listen to them?
5 List the different types of communication which children can be made aware of.

BODY LANGUAGE

What is body language?

Body language is a complex system whereby information about feelings and emotions is communicated to others by bodily movement and posture, and without the use of words (non-verbal communication). Researchers' estimates of how much of what we want to convey is transmitted through body language vary between 50 and 70 per cent. Some of our body language we are conscious of, but most of it is unconscious. If the 50–70 per cent estimate is correct, we take in a staggering amount of information from this source. Children learn about body language from the adults in their environment. We take it for granted that much of it is learned in an unconscious way, though we do encourage them, for example, to wave 'bye bye' and give hugs. Adults are much more concerned about the development of children's oral language.

Eye contact is our most powerful tool for communication, yet we are usually not aware of the kinds of messages our eyes send. It is interesting however that we cannot usually cope with more than intermittent eye contact (five seconds out of every 30). More than that makes us feel uneasy.

<table>
<tr><td>

DO THIS!

What might the following mean:

a) A person stands with palms up and hands held out?

b) Hands are thrown in the air?

c) Raised eyebrows?

d) Shrugging shoulders?

e) Clenched fist?

f) Shaking head while at the same time saying 'Yes' in Britain?

</td></tr>
</table>

Information about feeling and emotion can be conveyed without the use of words

The study of movements of the body and their communicative function is called kinesics. This word is often used interchangeably with paralinguistics. Such things as facial expression, head and eye movements as well as gestures all support, emphasise or give particular shades of meaning to what is being said. Some linguistic studies have shown that there is a pattern and structure to these movements in the same way that there is a pattern and structure to the sounds which when put together make up speech.

A consideration of body language includes some or all of the following:

- facial expressions
- movements of the head
- movements of the hands
- position of the body
- **proxemes**
- appearance
- tone of voice
- pitch of voice
- speed of answers
- length of pauses

DEFINITION

proxemes the physical distance between people when they are talking to each other, as well as their posture and whether or not there is physical contact during their conversation

- length of silences
- use or non-use of touch.

No doubt you can add to this list.

In addition, vocal **paralanguage** needs to be taken into account. This refers to the thousands of ways in which any word can be said which adds emphasis or other subtle meanings to the words. Paralanguage includes:

- pitch
- intonation
- regional accent
- sarcasm
- hesitations
- emotion
- the way in which stress is distributed over utterances.

Again you can probably add to this list. Vocal paralanguage is a very powerful, essential and subtle part of human communication. It also gives our listener cues about our background, identity, feelings and the kind our person we are.

The effect of body language is more powerful in some situations than others. An example of this is when somebody is lecturing or teaching. We need a lecturer to use appropriate non-verbal communication, especially eye contract, otherwise we quickly lose interest.

Cultural differences

It is important to be aware of cultural differences in body language. We may fail to understand people from other cultures even though they are speaking the same language as us because their gestures, expressions and emotions may be different. Culture may govern:

- how we stand when we are talking to others
- how we use or avoid eye contact
- how touch is used. There are patterns of touch such as lightly touching an arm to denote support or friendship
- how close or far away we stand or sit from others
- how we express or suppress powerful emotions such as joy, anger, etc.
- the type of body contact we can appropriately have with young children.

Certain non-verbal signals may have different meanings internationally. An example of this may be a thumbs-up sign which means 'good luck' in the UK, but is an obscene sign in Iran. Japanese people have traditionally been uncomfortable with handshakes or other forms of physical contact in public and have a system of bowing instead.

Non-verbal traits may lead to the development of stereotypes which can be damaging to people. Italian people are more facially expressive and gesture more when they talk than British people. It would be unfair to label Italians 'excitable' and the British 'cold' because of this.

DEFINITION

paralanguage the many ways in which a word can be said, including the use of gestures, eye movements, tone of voice, used to add emphasis and meaning to

Children's non-verbal communication

The development of a baby's non-verbal communication skills is very interesting to observe and essential to the later development of verbal communication. Wood (1992) says that 'Verbal communication is deeply rooted in patterns of pre-verbal communication'. This pre-verbal communication has a role in helping the very young baby and an adult achieve mutual understanding. An adult with a 4-month-old baby on his lap will frequently observe the direction of the child's gaze and then follow it, linking it to some verbal act like naming the objects looked at. By 8 months babies are becoming responsive to the various features of paralanguage – perhaps different types of intonation or pitch. By being responsive to an infant's facial expressions, gestures and intonations, familiar adults help to ensure that communication is in place before the child actually begins to speak.

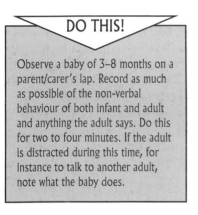

DO THIS!

Observe a baby of 3–8 months on a parent/carer's lap. Record as much as possible of the non-verbal behaviour of both infant and adult and anything the adult says. Do this for two to four minutes. If the adult is distracted during this time, for instance to talk to another adult, note what the baby does.

Very young children use gesture to communicate

Children develop a fluency of gesture as they develop language. An uneven pattern of development of non-verbal skills is usually present in children with autism (Chapter 9, page 168) and other language disorders. The more observant we are of children's non-verbal communication, the richer our overall communication with them will be.

✔ PROGRESS CHECK

1 What is considered to be our most powerful tool for communication?
2 Give some examples of vocal paralanguage.
3 Which aspects of non-verbal communication might be influenced by cultural differences?
4 Why is it important that a parent/carer is responsive to a infant's non-verbal communication?

COMMUNICATION THROUGH ART, MUSIC, DRAMA AND DANCE

This book is about language and literacy – the two forms of communication which we are going to look at most. However, there are other ways of communicating that are important for children and will, in addition to giving them opportunities to express ideas, emotions and feelings, help them to develop language and literacy skills. These are art, music, drama and dance.

Visual arts

Art is a creative, human skill. It involves representing thoughts and feelings and understanding of a subject in a variety of ways. Art can be anything from a young child scribbling on a misty window pane to the world-famous works of the old masters. We need to respect all means of communication and representation, and art is no exception.

We know very little about the beginnings of art just as we know very little about human beings in prehistoric times. It is likely that the earliest people did not think of their art as something nice to look at. Rather it was something powerful to use. The oldest cave paintings of animals – reindeer, bison and wild horses – were vivid and lifelike, but they were often put randomly on top of each other and sometimes they were deeper in caves than it is thought people might have lived. It is possible that people thought that by drawing the animals it gave them power over them and made it easier for the animals to be hunted and caught. They were representing (and communicating) the most important thing in their existence – the need for food to survive.

It is likely that any form of visual art – painting, drawing, sculpture, pottery, photography, cinema – and other graphic and pictorial means of creating pictures and objects involve us in communicating some or all of the following:

- representing a view of something that is uniquely different from anyone else's point of view. When studying the art of others, we spend much of our time discussing their view of what is represented

- our feelings and emotions. Sometimes what is painted or drawn may not be as important as the need to express feelings like anger, calmness, sadness or a sense of beauty

- our need to be in control. Just as the earliest known paintings were produced to gain some sort of superstitious control over animals to be hunted, so our creations may also give us a sense of control over our environment.

Art as a tool of communication comes into its own when it is used by young children who have not yet developed enough language to communicate their thoughts, emotions and feelings. It is also extremely important when there is any degree of communication difficulty.

> **THINK ABOUT IT**
>
> What might a 4-year-old child be communicating when she paints a picture?

> **THINK ABOUT IT**
>
> How can children benefit from discussing their art work with adults?

GOOD PRACTICE

- Respect children's art as a valid means of communication. Ensure that you are familiar with the stages and sequence of children's development in drawing and painting.
- Develop the analytical skills necessary to understand children's art.
- Provide children with the means to express themselves through a wide variety of art techniques – provide materials like paints, clay, collage materials and the space where children can use them.
- Encourage children to discuss their art work. This requires skill. Asking a child what she has drawn may put her off – to her what she has drawn is obvious.
- Give children the language and vocabulary to discuss art – words like shade, tone, tint, shape, curve.
- Be careful about praise. Telling a child that a picture is beautiful may raise self-esteem, but if this is said every time it can become meaningless. Praise effort, for example the time spent selecting colours. Be honest and positive. Tell a child what you particularly like.
- Give children the opportunity to examine and appreciate the art work of others. Looking at the work of older children can be as valuable as visiting an art gallery, but they need to have both experiences..
- Discuss with children the pros and cons of different types and sizes of paint brushes and modelling tools and how they are best used. Discuss the many different ways paint can be mixed.
- Introduce visual arts from other countries. This develops an understanding and appreciation of other ways of using colour and other forms of representation. It may also reinforce the cultural identity of some of the children that may be in your care.
- Be aware of the cultural diversity of the children you are working with. There are cultural differences in the colours people might select and the type of art they are exposed to.

Music

Sounds arranged in patterns that are pleasant to listen to are called music. To feel that patterns of sounds are music, we need to appreciate them and also identify them as music. There is no universal acceptance of what is music. Metal scraped on concrete, even if arranged in patterns, may jar the senses of many people, but be considered as music by others. The sounds which make up music can be made by the human voice or by the vast array of musical instruments which humans are capable of playing. The sounds made can be long or short, high or low, loud or quiet. Played together and arranged in patterns that are pleasing to our ears, we have something we call music.

Like visual art, music is capable of communicating both our conscious and subconscious thoughts. As with any other communication system, for communication to take place both the music maker and listener must understand, at some level, the code used. As adults we know the kind of music that excites us, makes us sad, relaxes us and so forth. Within a culture people share an understanding of the type of music they associate with different feelings.

As with visual art, music is an essential ingredient in the lives of young children. It gives them another medium through which they can express and communicate feelings and emotions. It develops in them an awareness of sound which helps with the development of language and literacy. It is a particularly valuable tool for children who have special needs which impair other forms of communication.

Adults are often put off introducing children to music because of mistaken belief that they somehow have to be musically talen themselves before they can teach children. A large proportion of stu report that they find initiating musical activities, even simple n

DO THIS!

Obtain some music from another culture that you have not consciously listened to before. Listen to it and be aware of any difficulties you have in understanding what it might be intending to convey.

rhymes, the most difficult thing to do. This is a pity because even the least musical person can introduce children to the world of music in the most exciting ways if they only believe they can.

GOOD PRACTICE

- Children need to be introduced to the fundamental activities involved in music – performing, composing and listening.
- Integrate musical activities into other areas of learning. For example, songs or rhymes can be used to reinforce the learning of new vocabulary introduced in a story.
- Introduce children to all types of music – pop, classical, opera, jazz, and many other types.
- Give children the opportunity to hear music from many cultures.
- Provide music for them to dance and move to.
- Use programme music occasionally – music that has a story. Prokofiev's 'Peter and the Wolf' is a good one to start with. Children will be more inclined to listen if they know the story first.
- Have as wide a variety of musical instruments available as possible. Show children how to use them and give them opportunities to experiment with them on their own and with others. Have adult- directed sessions sometimes.
- Spend a short time each day listening to a piece of music. This can be therapeutic for everyone and develop children's listening abilities. Briefly introduce the music first. When they are familiar with this routine, the children can suggest what they want to listen to. Occasionally encourage them to give reasons for their choice.
- Provide music that is considered to be sad, haunting, lively, stately, and so forth. Give children the necessary vocabulary to discuss the music they are listening to.
- Provide opportunities for the children to make sounds, starting with simple clapping and joining in with singing rhymes and songs, leading onto exploring sounds with all types of instruments.
- Where possible, invite adults to play instruments for the children. Don't forget electronic instruments or a visit to a church to hear a church organ being played.
- Encourage children to listen to sounds in the environment – birdsong, traffic noise, weather noises, etc.
- From time to time organise instrument-making activities where simple shakers and rubber-band instruments can be made by the children. Always make sure that they are used afterwards and the sounds they make discussed.

For child-care practitioners and teachers the list of ideas is endless, and there are many books and magazine articles which give new ideas and encouragement. There are also many excellent training programmes like the one being piloted by the English National Opera Baylis Programme. These resources will help you to encourage children to listen to and enjoy music, and to let music communicate some of the richness of the world to them.

Give children opportunities to explore a wide range of musical instruments

Drama

The value of drama as a communication tool is well known. If we use the term role-play instead of drama, we have a better understanding of how it works as a means of communication. Role-play is something children spontaneously indulge in from an early age and, if used, it is a useful learning and communication tool at all stages of a person's education. For instance, role-play is often included in management training courses. Its value lies in the fact that it allows the participants to practise expressing a variety of thoughts, feelings and emotions in a relatively protected way.

Role-play is a valuable part of children's learning. Sometimes the way a play area is set up encourages role-play round a particular theme, for example doctors and hospitals, or it may give the children the opportunity to spontaneously role-play and therefore communicate what is important to them at that moment. Through their role-play they can:

- develop their language and literacy skills
- reinforce previous learning about events and situations in their lives
- come to terms with painful and unpleasant realities that they may have been exposed to, for example, hospitalisation or separation of parents
- gain information about a variety of subjects. Dressing up in clothes from other cultures allows children to gain experience of that culture
- communicate their thoughts and feelings in a way that would not be possible through the use of language at that stage of their development
- learn the skill of interacting with others
- become aware of the needs of others
- rehearse familiar stories
- explore skills and interactions that they are unlikely to be able to experience directly.

Adults who value drama or role-play as a rich communication tool have the responsibility to provide children with:

- the space and time to role-play
- a rich variety of props, that are developmentally appropriate, to encourage all types of such play
- an environment where stereotypes are challenged
- content areas which reflect cultural diversity
- opportunities for children to work collaboratively
- the possibility of integrating other areas of learning, such as speaking, listening, reading and writing in role-play sessions
- opportunities for developing their imaginative abilities through exposur to a variety of stories
- opportunities to see drama performed by older children and occasion by visiting groups.

Give children a variety of props to aid their role-play

Dance

Dance and any other form of movement are ideal for encouraging children to communicate using their whole bodies without the aid of speech. It allows them the opportunity the make use of their creative energies to express feelings and emotions. If supported and encouraged in the early stages, children will learn to use this mode of expression in uninhibited ways.

Children should be given the opportunity to:

- move to music in a variety of ways
- enjoy movement
- see different types of dance – ballet, disco, ballroom, and any others
- enjoy dance from a wide range of cultures.

✔ PROGRESS CHECK

1 List three things that may be communicated through visual art.
2 Why is it necessary to be careful about spontaneously praising all children's art work?
3 What are the fundamental music activities children need to be introduced to?
4 List three ways that children can be introduced to music.
5 What is the value of role-play as a communication tool?

FURTHER READING

Fromkin, V. and Rodman, R. (1993) *An Introduction to Language*, 5th edition, Harcourt Brace College Publishers
This textbook assumes no previous knowledge on the part of the reader. It is nevertheless an in-depth study of language and would be suitable for students on level 4 courses and first-year undergraduate programmes.

Fast, Julius (1971) *Body Language*, Pan
This book gives an account of how to understand body language.

Whitehead, David (1996) *Teaching and Learning in the Early Years*, Routledge
The chapters covering individual curriculum areas are very good.

Wood, David (1992) *How Children Think and Learn*, Blackwell
How children think and learn in the Early Years is explored in this book. It is suitable for students on advanced courses or any student who wants to consider this area in depth.

Theories of language development

PREVIEW

The key topics covered in this chapter are:

- How is language studied?
- Behaviourist approaches to language development
- Innate theories of language development
- Social interactionist approaches
- Language and thought.

Language is a complex human behaviour that is not yet fully understood, but we do know that it is a system of symbols which we use to communicate with each other about our world. A question which concerns anyone interested in children's language development is how they are able to complete the complex task of language acquisition in such a short period of time. Many theories have been put forward and continue to be actively debated. Studying the different theories of language development will help you to think about how children might acquire language and also develop your own views on the subject.

THINK ABOUT IT

Language is a complex human activity. If you wished to study the language development of young children, think of some of the ways you would approach this task.

HOW IS LANGUAGE STUDIED?

The way language has been studied has depended on:

- the technology available at different times
- what researchers, linguists, psycholinguists, psychologists and educational professionals have needed to know about particular aspects of language and communication

- availability of funds needed to carry out the research
- prevailing theories of language acquisition.

During the last 30 years, methods of studying language and communication have become more sophisticated and accurate. They are now more creative, effective and elegant as they have built upon the methodology, new technology, and knowledge from previous research.

Methodology

There are various ways to collect information about how children develop and use language. The methods used depend very much on the type of information required. These may include:

- anecdotal records
- diaries
- observations.

Anecdotal records

An anecdotal record is a record of an event that has already happened. The researcher has to rely on the memory of the person recording the event. Such records are usually short accounts of a child's speech – words, **grammar**, sentences or content. These are often collected by parent/carers, teachers or other professionals and they can be used to provide a focus for further studies. The advantages of anecdotal records are that they can be:

- used to give an overall picture of a child's stage of language development
- spontaneously done when something interesting or relevant is taking place
- easily done – they may only require the recorder to jot down a few notes
- good for giving an overall picture which takes the context in which the language is used into account.

The disadvantages are that:

- they may not be fully accurate
- they may be **subjective**
- observers sometimes see what they want to see.

Diaries

These can be the basis for **longitudinal studies** which show the development of a child's language over time. They are usually kept by parent/carers and samples of a child's speech are entered daily, bi-weekly or weekly. A researcher will usually visit at regular intervals to discuss and record details of context so that a better overall picture can be obtained.

Diaries can be kept by parents/carers and written in regularly

The advantages of diaries are that:

- they are inexpensive to do
- they show change over time
- the context in which language is spoken can be recorded, which is a further aid to understanding
- they can be used to record a child's use of language in a home environment, when he is relaxed and does not feel under any pressure to perform.

The disadvantages are that:

- they require a lot of discipline and routine
- they could be subjective
- parent/carers may want to give a better impression of their child's language than they feel the language recorded gives, so there may be a tendency add an extra word or phrase here or there.

Observations

Observations can be used to record accurately a child's stage of language development. They can be:

- single narrative observations lasting for short periods of time, for instance 3 to 20 minutes
- event samples, where the observer writes down what a child says on a particular occasion, for instance, a new situation or when he is communicating with another child
- time sample observations, where the observer listens and records what a child says at regular intervals, for instance, every hour from 8 a.m. to 5 p.m. over a three-day period
- checklists. A list of expected speech features can be made, and this list can be used once, or at intervals, to check how many of the features listed the child has acquired. Checklists can form part of longitudinal studies.

It is important to observe children discreetly

Observations are useful for getting a quick picture of a child's language and communication skills. They are used in nurseries and classrooms to increase a practitioner's knowledge and understanding of individual children's stages of development. They are also completed for record-keeping purposes. The advantages of observations are that they:

- are useful to get a quick picture of a child's current state of language development

- are inexpensive

- are easy to complete, after the observer has some initial training in the correct method of recording observations

- can be completed anywhere as long as the observer has a notebook.

The disadvantages of observations are that it can be:

- difficult to hear everything that a child is saying – individual words or phrases can be unclear to the listener

- sometimes difficult to write quickly enough to record everything that a child is saying

- inhibiting or distracting for a child if they see someone observing them.

Audio recordings

Using a tape recorder can sometimes ease some of the problems that may occur with written observations. A tape recorder can be left near a child's cot to catch early morning **monologues** or in the home area of the nursery where a number of children of the same age are playing together. This is often a way of capturing the diversity and range of language achievement that may be normal within a particular age-range. Tape recorders can be placed in unobtrusive positions so that the children do not know they are being monitored. For research purposes, small radio recorders can also be strapped onto children as they go about classroom activities. The development of bilingual children's language can be monitored in this way.

CASE STUDY

Elena

Elena started at the nursery when she was 3. From the beginning she spent her time going from activity to activity. At first, the staff were content with this, feeling that she was settling down. They gradually became aware that she rarely interacted with other children and that her responses to them were usually a nod or shake of her head. However, she did not give them any trouble and since they were, at the time, coping with several hyperactive and aggressive children, they told themselves that it was early days yet and that she needed more time to settle. After three weeks, they discussed her at a team meeting since her key worker was becoming very worried. There were mixed views as to whether anyone had seen her communicate with another child and no one was sure they had actually heard her speak. Anecdotal observation was that she communicated, but non-verbally. They were sure she could speak as they had heard her chatting to her mother. It was decided to observe Elena formally during the following week using a time sampling method. Her position in the room, who she was with at the time and any language being used, were to be recorded for 2 minutes every hour on the hour from 10 a.m. to 2 p.m. from Monday to Thursday. On Friday the findings were analysed by her key worker and two other members of the team. The observations showed clearly that Elena was always on the fringe of a quiet group who usually ignored her. She was never in a position where there was an opportunity for her to communicate and staff members only rarely spoke to her. It was decided that time would be set aside to talk to Elena without insisting on verbal replies. She was encouraged to play with a small group of quiet children and, within the context of the activity, the other children were made aware of what she could do. Within two months Elena had no problems entering a group and could communicate. She was also very happy to chat to staff members though she continued to prefer quieter children and would only enter noisier groups if an adult was present.

1 Should the staff have started formally observing Elena sooner? Give reasons for your answer. Discuss this with someone in your staff team or student group.

2 Would two or three narrative observations of 5 minutes duration have been of any use? Give reasons.

3 Apart from her lack of communication, what other information did the time sampling method yield which was useful for the staff team when planning their strategy to help her?

Video recordings

Video recordings provide a researcher with considerably more information than the previous methods described. They may include details of:

- eye-contact
- hand movements
- other body language

Remember to obtain permission from parents/carers before recording or videoing children

- the context in which the language takes place
- other children present
- adults present
- toys and equipment available
- distractions.

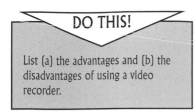

DO THIS!

List (a) the advantages and (b) the disadvantages of using a video recorder.

Video recordings can provide an observer with much information

DO THIS!

Choose a 4-year-old child who is particularly talkative.

a) At the end of your nursery day write a short account of the child's speech using examples of things you heard him or her say during the day. This would be an anecdotal observation.

b) Next day do a formal observation for 3–5 minutes of the same child using language. You can either write it or use a tape recorder.

c) Compare your anecdotal account of the child's language with your observations. Did the observation highlight anything which you hadn't previously noticed?

The advantages you probably identified in the exercise above may have included having an accurate picture of what is happening which can be played back several times and analysed. Under disadvantages you probably listed such things as intrusiveness and having the time to make the recording.

Types of research

In the previous section we looked at a variety of methods that researchers use to obtain information about how individual children speak. Sometimes researchers use this information as part of a research study which is designed to increase our knowledge about children in general rather than on an individual child. The following types of study may enable them to understand the development of children's language and communication:

- animal studies
- longitudinal studies
- cross-sectional studies
- laboratory studies
- cross-cultural studies

Animal studies
Such studies have been carried out to see if:

- language is an uniquely human activity

23

- it is possible to understand what is really meant by 'language'
- more can be learned about the social and cognitive processes involved in learning a language
- more understanding can be gained about whether language is something we are programmed to use at birth.

Animal studies may take the form of teaching animal primates (the highest order of mammals, which includes monkeys, apes and humans) to talk. Sometimes chimps are reared from birth with human children. Since animals have not got the same voice-producing mechanisms as humans, they are physiologically unsuited to producing human speech and all attempts to teach them to speak have, so far, produced limited results. Some progress was made with Washoe who was taught American Sign Language. Chimps have high manual dexterity and using sign language was an innovative and very interesting idea. It was claimed that Washoe learned 200 words, including nouns, verbs, adjectives and pronouns. Washoe was also socialised in that she was brought up as a human child from a 1-year-old. Activities such as toilet training, eating and playing and other children's activities were all part of her day.

Longitudinal studies

A longitudinal study is a study that takes place over an extended period of time. The main aim is usually to increase information about rates of language development, the order of the stages of language development, or the effect of different settings, for instance, home, day nursery or school, on how language develops. Such studies have clear purposes, such as to study whether there is a difference over time between the language used at home or at school, or perhaps whether there are specific linguistic skills that are important for success at school.

The well-known Bristol Study on 128 children conducted by Gordon Wells over a period of ten years, in the 1970s and early 1980s, was one such study. The children were studied from shortly after their first birthdays until the end of their primary schooling. The aim was to consider the major linguistic influences on children's educational achievement. Observations, tests, assessments, interviews with parents, teachers and the children themselves were used to achieve this.

Longitudinal studies, especially those carried out over a fairly long period of time have the disadvantage of children dropping out because of changes of school, illness and other life events. They always need careful planning and budgeting. Their advantages are that the same subjects are compared with themselves, so there is no need to match subjects for **variables** such as age and type of school. Longitudinal studies also provide opportunities to study the effects of life events, such as illness, change of school, separation of parents, on, for instance, language development.

Cross-sectional studies

In a longitudinal study the language of a child or group of children may be studied over an extended period of time. In a cross-sectional study, a number of individual children, or groups of children, of different ages may be studied at the same time. The groups or individuals are matched on all the variables which might influence the behaviour or ability being studied. These include gender, race, social class background and intelligence.

THINK ABOUT IT

Think about a possible longitudinal study which could be carried out in your present placement to research some aspect of language development.
If you are doing this as part of a group, discuss your thoughts with the group.

DEFINITION

variable any feature of the testing or observation that is apt to vary, for example the amount of light in a room or the words used by the researcher to ask a question

---

The advantages of a cross-sectional study are that:

- it can be relatively easy and quick to carry out
- it is short term and therefore is likely to be inexpensive
- data (the facts gathered from studies) do not need to be stored over a long period of time as in the case of longitudinal studies
- subjects are less likely to drop out when a study takes a short time to complete
- it provides age-related **norms**.

The disadvantages of cross-sectional studies are that:

- there can be differences between individuals or groups studied which would make the study of a particular item, such as language, difficult to compare
- it is often difficult to match subjects in this type of study.

Laboratory studies

These are studies conducted under controlled conditions in a laboratory and are usually only used with babies. They are often designed to consider one aspect of communication, for example, turn-taking in young babies' communication with their mothers. All possible distractions, for instance noise and movement, are removed, so that the specific aspect of language or communication being studied is not interfered with. If a number of children are to be tested, all variables are controlled so that, as far as possible, extraneous events, such as noise, the meanings of the words used or the position of the tester, do not influence the results. Laboratory studies are useful to focus directly on a specific aspect of language, but since most language happens in the context of a social setting many linguists feel that laboratory studies give only part of the picture.

Cross-cultural studies

Cross-cultural studies compare the language and communication of children in different cultural settings. One result from such studies is the information that has been provided about the universal nature of the stages children go through while progressing from early language to adult communication – it is now known that children in most societies go through the same stages in the same sequence when developing language. A study carried out by Dan Slobin in 1975 looked at children in more than 40 cultures to see if they used common strategies to learn language. He found that this was so as, for example, children in all languages paid attention to the ends of words when they were learning to talk.

Cross-cultural studies can also take place within a specific community, such as a nursery school, where there are children from diverse cultural backgrounds who may be exposed to different languages at home from that used at school. Such studies have been used to enhance our knowledge and understanding of many aspects of language development.

✔ PROGRESS CHECK

1 What technology has become available in the last 30 years which has made it possible to find out much more about how children develop language?
2 What might be the disadvantages of written observations of language and/or communication?
3 In what ways can animal studies help our understanding of language development?
4 What is a longitudinal study?
5 Explain the difference between a longitudinal study and a cross-sectional study.
6 What are cross-cultural studies?

BEHAVIOURIST APPROACHES TO LANGUAGE DEVELOPMENT

What are behaviourist theories?

Behaviourist theories (also called learning theories) of language development stem from the ideas of B.F. Skinner (1904–96). Skinner devised the idea of **reinforcers**. When a baby first starts making cooing sounds the mother is delighted and shows her approval by behaviours such as smiling and repeating the sounds back to the baby. The baby enjoys the attention and learns that vocalising gets this positive attention. The positive attention is said to reinforce the baby's behaviour. If the mother stopped showing delighted behaviour when the baby cooed, the baby might stop vocalising and the behaviour is then said to have become extinguished.

Skinner argued that these dependent relationships between behaviour and subsequent environmental events control language development and changes during childhood. Adults do all of the following with their children. They:

- interact with children
- respond positively to attempts at communication
- encourage the association of words with events, for instance, the sounds *da da* when a child's father appears
- name objects and events
- reinforce meaningful speech.

Appropiate input helps children learn to speak and communicate. Adults also respond selectively to their children's vocalisations and communication and thus shape (i.e. gradually build up a particular behaviour through reinforcement) the way language is learned. Language is essentially a set of habits that the child learns through adapting to outside circumstances and researchers who follow this approach are said to take an **empiricist** point of view.

Reinforcement involves encouraging the association of words with events, such as the sounds da da *when a child's father appears*

Arguments in favour of behaviourist theories of language development

The arguments in favour of behaviourist theories of language development are as follows.

- Research does show that a behaviourist approach is efficient for producing changes in children's language.
- It is possible to apply strict laboratory and scientific testing techniques in order to prove whether behaviourist theories of language development are true or not.
- There seems to be no doubt that adults are sensitive to what is appropriate in children's language development. They can then model, reinforce and correct the child's language and hopefully achieve the desired aims.
- It is easy to apply to specific situations, such as when dealing with children who have special learning needs. A behaviour which needs to be acquired by the child can be broken down into small units and the child is given a reward, such as praise, for each unit completed.

Arguments against behaviourist theories of language development

The arguments against behaviourist theories are based on the fact that some researchers have proved that adults do not in fact behave in the way described above. If children learn language just by having correct speech reinforced by the adults around them, we should be able to observe adults consistently showing approval for correct pronunciation of words and correct use of grammar. In fact, when researchers have studied adult–child interactions, they have found that adults are more likely to reward the content and truthfulness of children's speech, rather than pronunciation and grammar. What has been observed by researchers is that:

- attempts by adults to correct mistakes in grammar and pronunciation make little difference
- when there are attempts to correct grammar and pronunciation this has resulted in rigid language patterns
- some words, for example, 'No' are clearly understood before they are said by the child
- irregular forms of English, for example, 'gived' and 'gooses' are not heard by children and are yet frequently produced
- children are able to combine the words they have learned to form original sentences.

It has also been observed that parents/carers tend to correct only the truth and meaning of children's utterances and not the grammar.

THINK ABOUT IT

Think about whether you feel that reinforcement of a child's utterances by an adult is the way a child learns to speak.

CASE STUDY

A conversation with Ben

Ben: Julie liked it when I gived her my sweet.
Adult: That was a kind thing to do.
Ben: Then I gived her a hundred sweets.
Adult: That's not true. You only had one sweet left.

1 Which aspect of Ben's communication was the adult correcting?
2 What was left uncorrected?
3 In what way does the above conversation support arguments against behaviourist theories of language development?

✔ PROGRESS CHECK

1 Using a behaviourist approach, give an example of how an adult might encourage language development in a child under 1.
2 Think of the use of the words 'Thank you' in some societies. How do parents get children to automatically repeat these words in the appropriate situations?
3 List two of the arguments in favour of a behaviourist theory of language development.
4 List two of the arguments against such a theory.
5 How can a behaviourist approach be used to help children with special learning needs?

INNATE THEORIES OF LANGUAGE DEVELOPMENT

What is an innate theory of language development?

An **innate** theory of language development (also referred to as a biological theory or a nativist theory) is one that proposes that a child is born with the structures which enable him to develop language. Noam Chomsky and other innate theorists suggest that very young children (1- and 2-year-olds) can only acquire language because they are born with the **predisposition** to do so. At a certain stage of physical maturity, children who have enough space pull themselves up to a standing position and some time later they learn to walk. Language also develops along maturational lines. Children start by using single words to name very familiar objects or people. As their understanding grows they then progress to using two words, then three words and later fully formed sentences, which they use to communicate with others in their social environment. Noam Chomsky called this predisposition to acquire language a Language Acquisition Device (LAD). Later he referred to it as Universal Grammars. The LAD possesses just enough innate knowledge for the child to learn the grammar of a language from what he hears in his environment in the first four or five years of life. This innate linguistic ability enables all children to learn those features common to all human languages because they are born with the predisposition to apply the rules of grammar, to use words, to create sentences and to learn meanings in whatever languages to which they are exposed.

Arguments in favour of an innate theory

- It provides an explanation for how a child can acquire a knowledge about language that allows him to produce and understand utterances he has never heard before.
- Children acquire the skill of using grammar so well at such a young age that it is difficult to believe that it happens just because of their exposure to the language environment.
- Babies' babbling before 6 or 7 months makes all the sounds that are necessary to speak any known language.

Arguments against an innate theory

- The theory is difficult to test.
- It does not explain why, if language is innate, it does not develop soon after children are mature enough to control their voices – at around a child's first birthday.
- Chomsky based his theory, in part at least, on the speed with which young children acquire language. Whereas they do acquire proficiency in the use of language at a very early age, it is now recognised that the full acquisition of words and syntax for expressing complex meanings takes much longer.
- The idea that children learn to use grammar correctly in spite of often hearing poor examples is now considered to be untrue.

The nature v. nurture debate

This has been a long-standing debate in the field of language development. Innate theories of language development are an example of a point of view that sees nature, i.e. predispositions which children are born with, as being the prime influence on their behaviour. In contrast to that point of view are behaviourist theories, which see children's behaviour as the result of influences in the child's environment (the world in which the child grows up) – nurture.

After nearly half a century we seem to be no nearer settling the argument. It is valuable to consider this debate from a historical point of view, but it is likely that strictly adhering to either side is not the way forward for any researcher who really wants to know how children develop language.

Many studies do show, however, that adults do seem to have an in-built tendency to teach their children language. The use of motherese provides a good example of this.

Motherese

Motherese, commonly known as baby talk, is also referred to as child-directed speech (CDS) or baby talk register. It is the way that adults, especially mothers, but also fathers and older children, talk to very young children. Chomsky considered this to be an example of the poor language input which children receive despite which they still manage to learn phonology and grammar efficiently. He called it a 'degenerate input' and the argument itself is sometimes referred to as 'the poverty of the stimulus' argument. What he and other innate theorists mean is that the language children hear most often when they are very young is far from ideal and unless they are able to make use of innate structures they will never learn to talk properly. There has been considerable research into motherese in the last 20 years and if we examine it closely we can see that it contains many features which may in fact be very helpful for language acquisition.

The characteristics of motherese speech are usually that:

- it is high pitched
- it is slower
- it has clear pauses
- it contains shorter sentences
- the sentences are highly repetitive – what is said is repeated rather than expanded or **reformulated**
- the vocabulary is concrete, that is it is restricted to the here and now and it contains only what the adult thinks the child will understand
- individual words may be simplified
- it gives special emphasis to the most important words in sentences
- there may also be key words at the end of phrases and these words are louder and more high pitched
- the context is important – adult speech contains more nouns when children are playing with toys and more verbs during non-toy play.

THINK ABOUT IT

We generally believe nowadays that it is important to talk to children, to listen to them and to develop their language in every possible way. If children are born pre-programmed to learn language and they are going to talk when they are ready, just like they are going to sit up and walk, should we make so much effort to develop their language?

DEFINITION

reformulated where some of the words used may be different, or in a slightly different order, but the message given is the same

Choose some or all of the following observations – they need only be very short. Use the list of motherese features on page 30 to analyse your observations.

a) Observe a parent/carer talking to a baby less than 1 month old.
b) Observe a parent/carer talking to a 7-month-old baby.
c) Observe an child – perhaps 7–9 years old – talking to an infant under 1 year old.

It is considered possible that such language stands a higher chance of being understood by young children. Babies as young as 2 days old can discriminate between motherese and adult-to-adult speech. The level of motherese is also tied to the age of the child, and changes as his comprehension grows. It is used less and less as the child understands more.

It is not certain, however, whether children actually need motherese. It appears to have a universal nature though it is not used in all cultures. Depressed mothers are often unable to use it. Yet all children learn language.

✔ PROGRESS CHECK

1 What does an innate theory of language development propose?

2 What does LAD mean?

3 Give two reasons why an innate theory of language development might be correct.

4 Explain the nature v. nurture debate.

5 Explain how some of the features of motherese might help a child to learn language.

6 Why does the use of motherese change as an infant gets older?

SOCIAL INTERACTIONIST APPROACHES TO LANGUAGE DEVELOPMENT

Social interaction theory

According to social interactionist theory, language development must occur in the context of meaningful social interactions. Infants and parents create a range of formats which form the basis of language. Infants cannot learn without the support of adults. Jerome Bruner in 1983 contrasted the idea of Chomsky's LAD with his own idea of LASS (Language Acquisition Support System). He felt that the adult–child pair, in working together on language, helps the child to work out the meaning of **utterances** which he hears.

In the social setting children are also exposed to:

> **DEFINITION**
>
> **utterance** producing spoken language, either words or sentences

- *Turn-taking* This is an important aspect of language as communication is not aided if we all talk together. This appears to begin at a very early age in feeding. Schaeffer analysed the way in which sucking occurs in bursts and pauses and mothers make use of the pauses to play, cuddle and talk to their babies (reported in his book, *Mothering*, Fontana, 1975) He also noted that mothers and babies rarely vocalise at the same moment. Later adults play peek-a-boo games which reinforce turn-taking with older babies.

- *Paying attention* This is essential in communication and it is also necessary for actually learning about meanings. The joint attention which has been noted with mother–child pairs seems to be important for early naming of objects. Schaffer (1975) has shown that with infants of 10 months, mothers allowed their attention to be directed by their infant's behaviour and they continually checked to see which way their infants were looking.

Joint attention is important for naming objects

- *Word meanings* A social setting is essential for this important and basic task of language learning. Children also learn meanings because adults help to keep them focused on a topic.
- *Progress in speech development* Researchers who studied mother–child inter-action and children's speech developmental progress at 6, 13 and 24 months of age found that the quality and growth of vocabulary was tied to frequent interactive responses from the mothers, regardless of the education and social class of the mother.

THINK ABOUT IT

Do you think that the ability to use the social skills that are necessary to learn language, such as establishing joint attention in young infants, is innate?

Social interactionists believe that, although biological and cognitive processes are also necessary for language acquisition, the main driving force in language development is the interaction with other human beings. These interactions must also be meaningful and even though motherese may be useful, it is the shared meanings as well as the ability to establish joint attention that is really useful in learning language.

It is difficult to argue that language development can take place without a social setting. Indeed, when children have been found who have been severely neglected and left for years without any (or with very limited) social interaction, they have been unable to produce more than grunts or shrieks. The few accounts of feral children, that is children who have been reared with animals in the wild, would seem to indicate that they can only make the sounds to which they have been exposed. For example, in his book published in 1974, Jean-Claude Armen describes a young boy who had been reared by a herd of gazelles in the Sahara Desert. The boy, who was aged about 10 or 11 when he was discovered, could only communicate using the signs and grunts of the gazelles.

However we must always keep in mind that it is unlikely that any one theory of how children develop language has the correct answer. Each one has something to offer and we must approach each one with an open mind.

✔ PROGRESS CHECK

1 What are meaningful social interactions?
2 Explain Jerome Bruner's LASS.
3 To what aspects of the social setting, such as turn-taking, are very young children exposed to, which might help them to acquire language?
4 Explain why meanings are the driving force which helps children to acquire language.

LANGUAGE AND THOUGHT

We have already looked at three different theories of language acquisition. Although, for clarity, they have been presented separately, it is important to remember that they each have something to offer us in our search for an understanding of how children acquire language. It is also important to bear in mind that all areas of development are interdependent. Thus, a child who has not developed socially will often also have delayed language skills. The inter-relatedness of language and cognition presents some very difficult questions.

What comes first – language or thought?

Are children able to think before they have the vocabulary necessary to arrange their thoughts? Or, before they have acquired the necessary language, are they already thinking human beings using a different code from the language code we know? Anyone who has watched an 8-month-old infant knows that his brain is processing events and objects in his environment. The following views have been expressed by:

- Piaget
- Chomsky
- Vygotsky.

Piaget

The Piagetian point of view is that cognitive development happens first during the **sensori-motor period** as a result of the child using his senses and interacting physically with his environment The cognitive development that takes place in this way helps a child to develop and use language which he hears in his environment. Children are not able to use sophisticated language skills until towards the end of the sensori-motor period (18 months–2 years) when they are able to represent the world symbolically. The first words often appear when a child makes his first symbolic action, such as offering a doll a pretend drink. The Piagetian view is that children already think before the onset of language.

Chomsky

The Chomskyian position is that language and cognition are independent. Chomsky believes that ability to develop thought structures is innate. To support this he would say that regardless of intellectual development, all children develop language in much the same way. This does not explain why some children are able to manipulate language and understand meanings much more efficiently and more quickly than others.

Vygotsky

Lev Vygotsky, a Russian educator/psychologist (1896–1934), whose ideas on how children learn have been very influential during the last 20 years, felt that there was a definite relationship between language and thought. However, based on his observations of children's early **egocentric** speech and monologues, he proposed that speech and thought have different starting points within an individual. In the very early stages of development (before 2 years), thought is non-verbal. Words are not symbols for the objects they name – rather they are part of the object itself. At about 2 years of age language and thought become connected and after that children's intellectual development is determined by their language.

> **DEFINITION**
>
> **egocentric** in Piaget's terms, being unable to take the point of view of another

Does language decide the way we think?

Significant attempts have been made in recent years to change the way we view certain people, for instance, women and people with disabilities, by changing our use of traditional terminology. For example, we now use the word *chairperson* instead of *chairman* and when talking about a person or child who has a disability we put the person first – we say *a child who is deaf* rather than *a deaf child*. In this way we focus on the child first rather than the disability, and are better able to meet that child's individual needs. If we believe that attitudes to some people in our society are tied to the way we use language to describe them, then we must believe that language can control our thinking processes and the way we perceive the world. This is known as the world view.

The Sapir–Whorf hypothesis

In the 1950s a linguist Edward Sapir and a fire insurance engineer and amateur linguist Benjamin Lee Whorf proposed the hypothesis that the language we use decides how we think and how we see the world. Whorf had spent years studying American Indian languages and he noted that when they had no word for something it didn't seem to exist for them in the same way that it did for people who had a label for the particular thing. The Hopi language had no word or grammatical construction for time so he concluded that they must have a completely different concept of time.

He also used the example of the Inuits who have many different words for snow and are therefore able to have a more complete concept of snow than we have. In summing up their views Sapir said:

> 'Human beings … are very much at the mercy of the particular language which has become the medium of expression for their society. … The fact of the matter is that the "real world" is to a large extent unconsciously built upon the language habits of the group.'

Arguments for and against this view have continued since it was first proposed and current research is not inclined to accept it. The present approach is that whereas the language we use does have an impact on the way we think it is only one of the factors that influences cognition and behaviour.

✔ PROGRESS CHECK

1 Cognitive theory believes that thought happens before language. Without language, how might a pre-verbal child think?

2 What are Noam Chomsky's views on the development of thought?

3 From Vygotsky's point of view, when do language and thought become interdependent?

4 Explain in your own words the Sapir–Whorf hypothesis.

5 Give at least two examples of how the language we use might affect the way we think.

6 What might the world view be of a group of people who had no word for time?

KEY TERMS

You need to know the meaning of the following words and phrases. Go back through the chapter to make sure you understand them:

egocentric
empiricist
grammar
innate
longitudinal studies
monologue
norms
predisposition
reformulated
reinforcer
sensori-motor period
subjective
utterance
variable

FURTHER READING

Davenport, G.C. (1995) *An Introduction to Child Development*, Unwin Hyman
  Chapter 7 gives an account of learning theory and social learning theory.

Bruce, T. and Meggitt, C. (1999) *Child Care and Education*, Hodder & Stoughton
  Chapter 8 , pages 241–8, gives an excellent account of the use of symbols and symbolic behaviour.

Harley, T.A. (1997) *The Psychology of Language: From Data to Theory*, Psychology Press
  This is an in-depth but readable account of up-to-date thinking on language acquisition.

Pinker, S. (1999) *Words and Rules: The Ingredients of Language*, Weidenfeld
  This is a useful, up-to-date book which would be helpful to students who want to consider further whether the idea of universal grammars can be accepted.

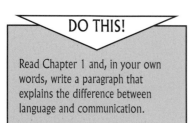

CHAPTER 3

The development of language and communication

PREVIEW

The key topics covered in this chapter are:

- The pre-linguistic stage (birth–1 year)
- The one-word stage (1 year–18 months)
- The first sentences (18–30 months)
- More complex sentences (30 months–3 years)
- Language in the over-3s
- The different uses of speech
- Summary of language development

The development of language in children is an amazing process. The helpless baby, who relies on crying to get her needs met, is transformed, within three or four years, into an individual capable of expressing complex thoughts and emotions through speech. Most babies who learn English appear to acquire language in a similar way, that is they appear to learn language in a predictable sequence. In this chapter we look at this process and think about the role of the child-care practitioner.

In this chapter we also look at the development of communication, rather than just looking at the development of language on its own. This is because it is clear that even new-born babies can communicate (rather effectively at times) although in the strict sense of the term they do not use language.

DO THIS!

Read Chapter 1 and, in your own words, write a paragraph that explains the difference between language and communication.

THE PRE-LINGUISTIC STAGE (BIRTH TO 1 YEAR)

Many people think that the process of learning to speak starts when a child is about 1 year old, when the first recognisable word occurs. However those of you who have experience of caring for babies will be aware that babies begin the process long before this.

In the *Think about it* exercise above, you probably thought about the way that the sounds a baby makes during the first year change, from gurgling and cooing, to babbling. You may also have thought about the way that children show that they sometimes understand what is being said, even though they cannot yet speak. The baby's ability to use gesture as a means of communication may also be regarded as part of the process of learning to use language.

The stage of developing language before the first word is uttered is called the **pre-linguistic stage**.

Early perception of sounds

For a child to develop verbal language she needs to be able to **discriminate between sounds**.

Babies can hear the difference between sounds before birth. New-born babies are able to hear as well as adults, except that they have more difficulty in hearing quiet, low-pitched sounds. Babies as young as 1 month old can tell the difference between sounds such as *p* and *b*, and *d* and *t*. They have also been shown to be able to tell the difference between sounds such as *bah* and *pah*. By the age of 6 months they can tell the difference between two-syllable words such as *bada* and *baga*.

The first sounds

Crying

Although a new baby can hear sounds, she is not so good at making them. In the first month the baby communicates through crying. She is totally dependent on an adult to meet her needs and having a good, strong cry gives her an excellent chance of survival. Parents/carers are soon able to tell the difference between the different kinds of cry that a baby makes. Most mothers will be able to tell the difference between a cry that indicates that a baby is hungry and one that tells her that the baby is in pain.

Small-for-dates babies, pre-term babies and babies with particular physical problems may have cries that are recognisably different from 'normal' infants. However new-borns who are deaf will cry in the same way as other babies.

Cooing

Somewhere between the ages of 1 and 2 months the baby will start to coo. **Cooing** usually occurs when the infant is happy and consists of vowel sounds, such as *uuuuu*. (A vowel is a speech sound made with the mouth open, i.e. not involving the lips or tongue, that corresponds to the letters *a, e, i, o, u*.) The baby may also laugh and gurgle. This coincides with the recognition by parents/carers of the first social smile. The infant develops a range of behaviours – smiling, crying, making eye contact and responding to her

THINK ABOUT IT

What aspects of a baby's behaviour, during the first year, shows that she is already beginning the process of learning to use language?

DEFINITIONS

pre-linguistic stage of language development in the baby's first year of life, when the baby develops sounds and gestures, before the emergence of her first words

sound discrimination the ability to hear the difference between sounds

DEFINITION

cooing sounds produced by babies at around 6 weeks of age, usually indicating pleasure, consisting of repeated vowel sounds mixed with laughing

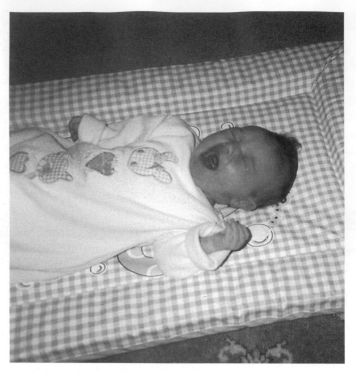

In the first month a baby communicates through crying

parents/carers – which are part of the attachment/bonding process between the baby and her regular care-givers.

Although the infant is not able to communicate verbally there are 'conversations' between the baby and parent/carer. The baby may react to an aspect of care by cooing and this prompts the adult to smile and talk to the baby. The baby may respond with eye contact and more vocalisations, which is rewarded by the adult smiling and talking back. It appears that adults from many cultures respond to young babies in the same way. They will talk in a high-pitched voice, raise their eyebrows, open their eyes wide and smile. Adults and babies enter into a 'conversation' where the baby will vocalise, pause and then the adult will reply.

The most satisfying 'conversations' for both adult and infant are those in which both baby and adult know each other well and they have had time to practise these exchanges so that they can pick up signals from each other and the 'conversation' goes smoothly.

This has important implications for child-care practitioners. It is now widely accepted that the key worker system is the most appropriate way of caring for young children in day-care establishments, especially babies. This is because the adult and baby must get to know each other very well for both social and language development to proceed. Adults caring for babies need to be sensitive and responsive so that satisfying interactions and relationships can occur and the baby develops a sense of emotional security.

A mother and baby communicating

Babbling

Until babies are about 6 months old they are unable to produce all the sounds necessary for speech. This is because their oral cavity and nervous system are immature. However, between 6 and 9 months babies have matured sufficiently to produce an increasing range of sounds. The baby begins to produce **babbling** sounds by combining consonant and vowel sounds, for example, *ma* or *dah*. (A consonant is a speech sound where the breath is partially obstructed by the tongue or lips. The sounds correspond to the letters *b, c, d, f, g, h, j, k, l, m, n, p, q, r, s, t, v, w, x, y, z*.)

When babies are about 7 or 8 months old, their babbling sometimes contains sounds not found in the language that they are hearing around them, but which can be found in other languages. However, by the time babies are 9 or 10 months old, these sounds have been lost and the babbling sounds more like the language they are learning.

In the babbling stage infants often repeat sounds, sometimes to amuse themselves when alone, as well as when they are with others. The repetition of syllables, for example, *mama* or *dada*, is known as a **reduplicated mono-syllable**. Although parents are often convinced that these replications mean Mummy or Daddy, this may not be so. It is not until infants are about 1 year old that vocalisations acquire meaning.

By about 11 or 12 months babies often repeat syllables over and over again. This is called echolalia, because the baby appears to be echoing herself.

During the babbling stage the speech of babies gradually begins to take on some of the intonation of the language they are being exposed to. Every language has a different sound contour. When we learn a foreign language

DEFINITIONS

babbling repeated sounds produced by babies when they are about 6 months old, consisting of vowel–consonant combinations

reduplicated monosyllable the repetition of a sound, for example, **mama**

as adults, we not only have to learn how to pronounce the individual words, but we also have to learn at what point in a sentence there is a rise or a lowering of intonation. Until we have learned to use correct intonation it will be obvious that we are speaking in a foreign accent. In the same way that a baby gradually changes the sounds she uses so that they are the ones found in the language she hears all around her, so she will gradually alter her intonation so that the babbling begins to sound more like the language to which she is exposed.

By about 9 months the babbling of a baby who is exposed to English is noticeably different from the babbling of a baby exposed to Spanish, for example, or Urdu, both in the production of sounds and in intonation. However if a baby is deaf, or is not exposed to language, then babbling does not change and can cease. This is due to a lack of stimulation and feedback from the environment.

Infants who are born to parents who are deaf and who are not exposed to oral language, but who are exposed to sign language, characteristically go through a sign babbling stage. Here vocalisations are replaced by gesture.

The use of gestures

In all babies, the use of gestures first appears at around 9 or 10 months when a baby begins to demand what she wants by using a combination of sound and gesture. An infant who wants you to give her a biscuit may stretch out her arm towards the biscuit, opening and closing her hand and vocalising loudly at the same time. As babies' motor skills develop you will notice that they point for things that they want using their index fingers. Some psychologists consider that the use of gesture is related to the development of the infant's understanding of grammar. Babies who point at an object and then look at their parent/carer appear to be 'saying' 'Look at that' or 'What's that?' The use of gesture and facial expression may reflect an understanding of how language works, before the child can use speech.

Babies begin to demand what they want by using a combination of sound and gesture

At this age infants will be able to play games like 'pat-a-cake' and will be able to wave 'bye-bye'. At the same time that babies acquire the ability to use gesture, they also begin to demonstrate that they can understand some words. For instance they may respond to their own name, stop what they

DEFINITIONS

receptive language the ability to understand the meaning of words

expressive language the ability to communicate verbally

are doing if they are told 'no', or respond to a request to 'look at the cat'. This ability to understand the meaning of words is called **receptive language**, whereas the ability to communicate verbally is known as **expressive language**.

The development of language depends on both innate characteristics and the influence of the child's environment. Parents/carers and child-care practitioners can, therefore, have a positive influence on a child's language development.

GOOD PRACTICE

- Ensure that a baby's hearing is checked as soon after birth as possible.
- From birth, surround the baby with language. Use routine care-giving activities, such as feeding and bathing, as opportunities to talk to the child.
- Be receptive; respond to the baby's vocalisations with smiles. Give the baby time to join in 'conversations' with you.
- Ensure that a baby in a nursery establishment has a key worker who can build up a relationship with her and be responsive to her so that satisfying patterns of interaction can occur.
- Sing to the baby. Research has shown that babies who are sung to tend to be more musical later on in life

- Don't have the radio or television on constantly in the background as this might delay language development.
- In day care or nursery have tapes of songs in the children's home languages. Try to learn some baby games in these languages.
- Young babies enjoy exploring books. Parents and carers can enjoy sharing books with babies from birth. Books should be strong, easy to wipe clean, with simple, bold, colourful pictures of familiar, everyday objects. The baby will enjoy sitting on your knee and being cuddled and held close as you read a book. She will not only increase her language and listening skills, but will also feel positive about the whole experience.

✔ PROGRESS CHECK

1 How well can a baby hear at birth?
2 How do new-born babies communicate?
3 How do babies communicate when they are about 2 months old?
4 What changes are seen at around 6 months?
5 How does babbling change at around 9 months?
6 What happens to the babbling of a baby who cannot hear?
7 When do babies start to use gesture?

THE ONE-WORD STAGE (1 YEAR–18 MONTHS)

At around 1 year of age a baby will produce her first word. Most parents and carers fail to recognise the baby's first word because it may not correspond to a word they know. The first word appears after the baby has begun to limit her babbling to the phonemes found in the language she is hearing, so the first word will consist of phonemes found in this language. However it may not correspond to a word or morpheme that is recognisable to adults. Often the baby makes up a word which consistently represents the same thing. The baby is seen to be trying to communicate using this word.

In the late 1970s the researcher Ronald Scollon recorded the first words of a baby called Brenda. Her first words included *da* for doll and *nene* which represented things like food or people that provided comfort. Brenda is famous now since you will read about her in most texts which describe language development.

A child's first words tend to be spoken in very specific situations. The infant may only produce them after a prompt, for instance, after being asked 'What's this?' There is a tendency to use the word in a very restricted way. For instance, a baby may use the word 'dog' to refer just to the family pet and not for any other dogs.

By 13 months some children are able to use words spontaneously in different contexts. The understanding that words can be used in a variety of contexts suggests the child is using the words as symbols and this indicates a leap in cognitive development.

The first words appear amongst the babbling. There is not an abrupt end to the babbling – the baby will continue to babble for about another six months. The use of non-word sounds in the older baby is sometimes referred to as **jargon**. The baby will often 'talk to herself' when playing with a toy or on her own.

Children who have no hearing have been shown to develop gestures that appear to represent an object or event (known as referential signs) at the same age that a hearing child develops her first words. This gives support to the idea that children are programmed from birth to develop a language in some form or other.

DEFINITION

jargon the use of non-word sounds in the older baby

GOOD PRACTICE

- When you recognise that a child is using a word correctly, make sure that you show the infant that you understand what she is saying.
- Encourage the child's receptive vocabulary by giving her instructions, for instance, 'Give me the ball' or 'Fetch the nappy'.
- Sing familiar songs to the child and encourage her to join in.

A baby will often talk to herself when playing with a toy on her own

Increasing vocabulary

When a child first begins to use words the process is slow. Each word is learned after many repetitions and it may take as long as six months to learn 30 words. However, some time in the second year, usually between 14 and 19 months, when a child is using about 50 words, there is an explosion in vocabulary. This pattern is not always seen. Some children continue to show a slow, steady acquisition of new words, but most children show this dramatic increase.

GOOD PRACTICE

- Give the child time to speak. Don't rush her – it is natural for small children to hesitate.
- Expand the child's vocabulary by using the names of things around you.
- It is important that you give eye contact to the child when you speak to her, and encourage her to look at you. This will help the child concentrate on what is being said.
- Share books, stories and rhymes with the child.

There have been many longitudinal studies that have looked at the characteristics of these new words. Most studies have indicated that early words are usually nouns (words which denote people, places or things), either referring to people, for example, *mummy*, or to animals or objects, such as *cup*. The nouns used are usually related to things or people that the child has an active involvement with, for instance, things children can play with, manipulate or eat. The use of 'verb-like' words appears later. (Verbs are action words, such as *go*, *see*, *eat*.) It is thought that this is because verbs describe the relationships between objects, rather than a single object. Cross-cultural studies tend to confirm the finding that children learn the words for people and things before they learn other parts of speech.

During this stage, the toddler learns to answer questions and she begins to comment on what she hears around her. She also uses her new vocabulary to take part in conversational exchanges with adults and older children.

CASE STUDY

Ben

Uchenna is the manager of a private nursery in the commercial area of a large city. Most of the children who attend the nursery have parents who are well-paid professionals and executives who work long hours and hold responsible positions. Ben is 6 months old, he is an only child and his mother, an accountant, is returning to work after a period of maternity leave. Ben attends nursery from 8 a.m. until 6 p.m. When he arrives home with his mother, there is only time for a brief playtime with both parents before it's time for bath and bed. Ben's mother decided to send Ben to the nursery instead of having a nanny because she wanted Ben to have the company of other children and she also feels safer knowing that the staff are well trained and supervised. However, she has expressed worries that group care may hinder Ben's language development.

1 As the manager, what decisions does Uchenna need to make about staffing that will affect Ben's language development?

2 What can Uchenna say to Ben's mother that will reassure her that Ben's language development will not be neglected in the nursery?

3 Ben's mother asks for Uchenna's advice as to what she can do at home to promote language development. What should Uchenna tell her?

✔ PROGRESS CHECK

1 Explain what a 'word' is. (Look back to page 3, if necessary.)
2 At what age do babies usually use their first word?
3 Why do parents sometimes fail to recognise the first word?
4 What part of speech are babies' first words?
5 At what age do some children show a sudden increase in vocabulary?
6 Why is it important to give babies eye contact when you speak to them?

THE FIRST SENTENCES (18–30 MONTHS)

Before a child uses two words together to form a sentence, she often uses one word on its own to represent a whole sentence. For instance, a 1-year-old baby might use the word 'milk' to mean 'I want my milk' or 'look at the milk'. The exact meaning may be understood by the context in which the word is spoken, the tone of voice or the gestures she uses. For instance, a toddler may say 'bottle' and reach out for it, opening and closing her hand. These one-word sentences are called **holophrases**.

Once a toddler begins to put two words together, it is possible to analyse the underlying grammar of the sentences. Psycholinguists who study the development of language in children traditionally divide the acquisition of grammar into two stages. From about 18 months until about 30 months the toddler uses short, simple sentences. This is known as **stage one grammar**. From about 30 months to 3 years the child uses longer, more complex sentences.

Stage one grammar

In the 1960s and 1970s the researcher Roger Brown observed many toddlers and identified the main characteristics of this stage of language development:

- Sentences are simple.
- Sentences are short.
- Sentences follow grammatical rules.

Sentences are simple

Sentences are simple because they lack what are called **grammatical markers** (also called **inflections** – the sounds added to a sentence that make the meaning precise). For instance, in English, if we want to talk about more than one dog we add an *s* to make *dogs*. This is described as using the plural form of a word and is an example of a grammatical marker. Other grammatical markers include using *-ed* on verbs to make the past tense, for example, *I climb* changes to *I climbed* in the past tense. The use of *'s* to show possession, for instance, *the dog's tail* is a grammatical marker, as is the use of auxiliary verbs, for instance the use of *didn't* in *he didn't come* or *is* in *He is climbing*.

Originally, research indicated that the lack of grammatical markers in toddlers' speech was universal, i.e. a feature of language development found in children all over the world. However, in languages such as Turkish, where grammatical markers (inflections) are more stressed, toddlers appear to use inflections earlier than children learning English.

Sentences are short

Because of the simple nature of the toddler's speech, it can sound like a telegram. Although no longer used today telegrams were a popular method of sending a message when few people had telephones in their own homes. The message was paid for by the word, so messages were kept as short as possible with only the essential words being used, similar to messages received by a pager. Brown described toddlers' speech as **telegraphic** because only key words, called **contentives** are used. Children in this stage use nouns, verbs and adjectives.

One interesting aspect of telegraphic speech occurs when a child is imitating an adult. If an adult asks the child to copy the sentence *Penny is singing to the dolls*, the child will probably say something like *Penny sing doll*. As well as being a good example of telegraphic speech, the sentence is interesting because of the six adult words the child only copies one of them in her sentence. This creation of new sentences, not heard before, has been used to suggest that children are using their own set of grammatical rules that are different from those of adults. It also indicates that any theory of language acquisition that relies on the child learning just by copying what adults say, must be an over-simplification.

The grammatical rules of early sentences

As indicated in the example given above, even when toddlers are using sentences of only one or two words, they are using 'rules' or grammar. The grammatical rules may not always be the same as for adult speech, but nonetheless sentence construction is not haphazard and follows a predictable sequence.

In the early 1960s, the researcher Martin Braine, investigated the grammatical rules that toddlers use. He found that some words were repeated often and always came in the same order in a sentence. He called these words 'pivot' words. An example would be the word *see*. A child would use it to make sentences such as *see Mummy, see dog, see milk*. The word *see* is a pivot word and always used before another word. Some pivot words may always be used in second place, for example, *want it*, *have it* and *touch it*.

'See dog'

Children are able to convey complex messages in sentences made up of just two nouns. Sometimes the same two-word sentence can have two different grammatical structures. One example, which is widely reported, was observed by Louis Bloom in the 1970s. Bloom recorded a child saying *Mommy sock* on two different occasions. On one occasion the child picked up the mother's sock and the sentence clearly indicated that the sock belonged to his mother. On another occasion the mother put the child's own sock on the child's foot. This time the sentence meant that 'Mummy is putting the sock on my foot'.

GOOD PRACTICE

- Be aware that as the child's parent or key worker you may need to translate what she is saying to others. Encourage the child to speak to other children and adults directly but if the message is unclear, help her out so that the experience is a positive one.
- Do not try to correct all of the errors that the child makes. Drawing attention to her speech may lead to problems later on.
- When the child talks to you using two- or three-word sentences, expand the sentences in your reply. For instance, the child may say to you **Daddy gone work** you could reply **Yes, Daddy has gone to work in his car**. Remember that the child learns how to speak from hearing the language spoken

around her. You need to be a good role model and take care about the way you speak when she is around. This is particularly important if you are a child-care practitioner. The parents will not like the child to pick up inappropriate vocabulary at nursery.
- Don't oversimplify your speech when talking to a toddler – use your normal way of speaking but slow down and try not to use long, complex sentences.
- Sharing books, stories and rhymes continues to be a great source of enjoyment and language development for both adult and child.

✔ PROGRESS CHECK

1 At about what age do children start combining words into simple sentences?
2 What is a holophrase?
3 What are the three main characteristics of stage one grammar?
4 What are grammatical markers?
5 Give an example of telegraphic speech.

MORE COMPLEX SENTENCES (30 MONTHS–3 YEARS)

DEFINITION

stage two grammar   the stage of language development when a child progresses from using simple, short sentences to using sentences that are longer and more complicated (roughly from 30 months–3 years)

When we looked at the way that toddlers learn new words we found that there was generally a slow start at the beginning and that most children show an explosion in vocabulary at around 18 months. In the same way children show a slow start in acquiring grammar, but sometime in their third year they show a sudden increase in the complexity of the sentences they use. This stage is described by Roger Brown as **stage two grammar**. Although the start of this stage has been given as 30 months, there is great individual variation. In this stage not only does vocabulary increase rapidly, but sentences are becoming longer and more complex. Researchers have found that there is an association between the size of a child's vocabulary and the complexity of the sentences that the child uses. This means that the larger the child's vocabulary, the more complicated are the sentences the child uses. By about 3 years of age a child may have a vocabulary of 1,000 words.

THINK ABOUT IT

Think of ways in which size of vocabulary and sentence construction could influence each other.

Changes that occur in stage two grammar

- The child begins to use grammatical markers or inflections.
- The child begins to use questions and negatives, words such as *no* and *not*.
- The child shows over-regularisation.

Using grammatical markers

When we looked at children who were using stage one grammar, we noted that they did not use grammatical markers in their sentences. During stage two these markers begin to appear.

Children don't suddenly use these markers all at once – their acquisition is gradual. Studies have shown that children usually add grammatical markers in a sequence that appears to be universal within each language, although there are variations between different languages.

In a study carried out in the 1970s Roger Brown identified the order in which children acquired grammatical markers:

1   the use of *-ing* added to a verb

2   prepositions such as *on* or *in*

3   the use of *s* to form plurals

4   irregular past tenses, for example, *sang* and *hit*

5   possessives, for example, *Debbie's hat*

6   the use of *the* and *a*, which are known as 'articles'

7   adding *s* to third person verbs such as *he wants*

8   regular past tenses such as *climbed* and *clapped*

9   the use of **auxiliary verbs** such as *I am singing*.

DEFINITION

auxiliary verb   a verb which is used with another verb in a sentence and which shows grammatical functions such as time or person, for example, **she IS working** or **they HAVE finished**

Questions and negatives

When children first start using questions they tend to make the same type of error consistently. It is as if they follow a set of rules, but not the adult rules of grammar. For example, when they first start to use questions beginning with words such as *when*, *who*, *what* and *where* children often get the words in the wrong order. For instance, they may say *Why it is laughing?*

In the same way, when children start to use negatives, they are able to use *not* to make a sentence negative, but are unable to use the auxiliary verb. They may say things such as *There no biscuits* instead of *There are no biscuits*.

Over-regularisation

Once children have learned a grammatical rule, they begin to incorporate it into their speech. This can lead to some characteristic errors, such as when the children start to use *s* to make plurals. Children may start referring to two sheep as *sheeps* or two feet as *feets*. This is a logical error and it will be some time before the children learn all the exceptions to the rule.

GOOD PRACTICE

- Encourage children to talk about activities and experiences that they have been involved in. Children of this age enjoy talking to the adults who care for them. However rushed you are, always have time to listen to children and show that you enjoy the conversations. If children are constantly being told to go away because you are busy they may stop trying to talk to you.
- Children will ask many questions, including questions about what words mean. Do not get irritated. This is an important stage of their learning. Be patient and answer their questions fully. Explain the meaning of new words and extend the children's vocabulary by using words they have not come across before.

- Children of this age enjoy the telephone. Give them the opportunity to talk to people they know on the telephone and give them an old telephone to use in their imaginary play. An old, real telephone will be much more satisfying than a toy one.
- Continue reading to children, and encourage them to join in. Ask questions which require a response from the children. For instance, don't just ask children to point things out, for example, **Where is the rabbit?**, but encourage them to enter into a conversation, for example, **Where is the rabbit going?** or **What has happened to the rabbit?**

Encourage children to join in

✔ PROGRESS CHECK

1 Describe common errors children make when they first begin to use questions and negatives.
2 Explain why a child who uses the word **sheep** correctly, starts to call them **sheeps.**
3 How can you extend a child's vocabulary whilst reading a story?

LANGUAGE IN THE OVER-3S

From 3 onwards, speech gradually becomes more complex and adult-like. Researchers have recorded children between 3 and 4 saying sentences such as: *I didn't catch it but Teddy did!*; *I'm gonna sit on the one you're sitting on*; *Where did you say you put my doll?*; *Those are punk rockers aren't they?*

Research has shown that children of this age are able to:

- use conjunctions like *and* and *but*
- combine two ideas together
- use embedded clauses
- make detailed observations about the world.

(A clause is a group of words that form a grammatical unit and contain a subject and a verb. An embedded clause is a clause that is put within a sentence, for instance, *that he got married* in the sentence *The news, that he got married, surprised his friends.*)

At the same time the child's vocabulary is increasing so that, at 4, a child typically has a vocabulary of about 1,500 words and a vocabulary of at least 2,000 at 5 years old.

As children grow older their understanding of the uses of language develops. They begin to understand social conventions, such as not interrupting others when they are speaking and using *please* and *thank you*.

Three-year-olds love to sing and talk. They can keep conversations going for several turns and 80 per cent of the time their speech is easily understood by all listeners. However they may have difficulty pronouncing the letters *r*, *l*, *s* and the *th* sound. Children of this age are able to talk about the future and can use words to describe shape, size, colour, texture, spatial relationships and the functions of objects. They can use words to describe what is happening, for example, *the big jet is flying high*. They are able to tell a simple story by looking at a picture.

As children become more proficient they discover the power of questions. They may continue to ask questions to which they already know the answer, as if they are using the question to test their own memory of the answer. In play they are able to use different voices for different roles.

Four-year-olds are increasingly able to talk in an adult fashion and are almost always able to be understood by adults who do not know them. They begin to be able to talk about feelings and ideas, and may be able to give long accounts of experiences that they have had. The 4-year-old will continue to ask a lot of questions.

Children may be able to give long accounts of experiences they have had

The older child

Throughout primary school children develop more difficult and complex sentence forms. For instance, they do not tend to understand passive forms of speech until they are over 6 years of age, and they will not use the passive form until they are much older. (The passive is where the object of a sentence becomes the subject. For instance, the sentence *The wind damaged the fence* becomes *The fence **was damaged by** the wind* in the passive form.)

The errors due to over-regularisation are no longer seen and infant mispronounciations disappear.

Once in the school system, fostering language development becomes part of the curriculum. Children of 4 who attend pre-schools and nurseries in England have a curriculum designed so that they can achieve certain goals on entry to formal education at 5 years old. Older children follow the National Curriculum.

GOOD PRACTICE

For 3- and 4-year-old children

- Encourage small groups of children to share their news in a 'circle time'. This helps children pay attention to what they are saying, helps them learn to take turns and helps them to see the purpose of language. Circle time also encourages children to listen to what other children are saying. Always show that you are interested in what the children are saying and show your pleasure and approval, even if the child doesn't quite manage to say what she intended.

- Sometimes encourage children to talk about their drawing and paintings. Even if you are not sure what it is that the child has drawn, avoid asking her directly what it is. It is more helpful to ask the child to tell you all about her drawing because it encourages her to put her ideas into words.

- Try to avoid using too many closed questions – those which only require a one-word answer, for instance, **Are you excited?**, to which the answer can either **yes** or **no**. Instead you should use open questions that require a longer, more thought out, response, such as **Why are you excited?**

- Listen carefully to children when they talk to you. Children often lose the 'thread' of a conversation and you will need to bring them back to the subject being discussed. If the adult is only listening with 'half an ear' the conversation may drift off into nonsense.

- Children sometimes need reminding to look at the person they are talking too. A child is easily distracted and may start looking about them when holding a conversation. Gently reminding them to look at you when they talk to you will help, and, of course, you should always look at them when you speak to them.

- Continue to answer all questions as fully and truthfully as you can, children are naturally curious and if you show that you are embarrassed or irritated they may stop asking you questions.

✔ PROGRESS CHECK

1 How many words does the typical 3-year-old child, 4-year-old child and 5-year-old child know?

2 At what approximate age can you expect a child to use the passive form of speech?

3 How does circle time benefit children's language development?

4 Why should you try to use as many open questions as you can when talking to children?

THE DIFFERENT USES OF SPEECH

So far in this chapter we have described the way that children typically learn to communicate using language. Language includes the use of speech and gesture, and can, of course, be written down. In this section we investigate how children learn some of the conventions that govern our use of one aspect of language – speech.

In your response to question 1 in the activity on the left you may have mentioned that speech can be used to:

- request or give information
- express feelings
- help build and maintain social relationships
- direct our actions (talking to ourselves).

This is not a complete list and you may have thought of other uses of speech.

In your responses to question 2 you may have thought of the following rules of conversation.

- Conversations involve taking turns, with each partner in a conversation being given time to express what she wants to say whilst the others listen.
- When someone is talking, the other partner(s) look at her.
- When someone begins to speak, she looks away from the other person. She looks at the listener again to signal that she is about to finish talking.

You may have thought of other 'rules'. Although it is not always easy to identify exactly what these rules are, you may have been in a situation where you are aware that there is something wrong with another person's conversational skills because the conversation does not flow.

Language pragmatics

As a child's language develops, so the way she uses it changes. The way language is used is called **language pragmatics**. During the pre-linguistic stage of language development babies appear to be joining in conversations with adults. They show that they have already developed skills in turn-taking and will gaze into the adult's eyes. If you observe the behaviour of a 9-month-old child, sitting in her high chair during a family mealtime, you can often see her 'following' the conversation as it flows around the dinner table. She moves her head to look at the person who is speaking and may 'join in' by vocalising. A child of this age is well on the way to being able to use the 'rules' of conversation.

By 18 months a child is able to use adult gaze patterns when having a conversation with others. And by the time she is 2 years old she is able to alter her speech according to the situation she finds herself in. In an example given by Helen Bee, a child may say *gimme* to another toddler as she grabs the toddler's glass of milk, but may say *more milk* when requesting a drink from an adult.

As children mature they are able to adapt their style of language more exactly to the person they are talking to. Four-year-olds have been observed using simpler speech patterns when talking to younger children compared to the complexity of speech that they use between themselves or with adults. At about 5 years of age children have been observed explaining something more fully to a stranger than a friend and are more polite to adults than their friends.

Language and self-control

Children often use language to direct or monitor their behaviour. In young children, self-directing speech is spoken aloud. At 2–3 years old children are often to be heard talking to themselves especially when playing on their own.

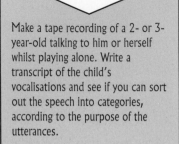

DO THIS!

Make a tape recording of a 2- or 3-year-old talking to him or herself whilst playing alone. Write a transcript of the child's vocalisations and see if you can sort out the speech into categories, according to the purpose of the utterances.

Children often use language to monitor their behaviour

You may have been able to identify the following categories when doing the activity above:

- instructions, where the child tells him or herself what to do
- commentaries, when the child describes what he or she is doing as they are doing it
- words or phrases designed to stop him or her doing something.

Theorists have put different interpretations onto this behaviour. Piaget considered that self-directing speech was caused because children of this age are egocentric (see page 34). The child's private language is considered to be evidence that the child is not yet thinking in the same way as an adult. However, Vygotsky thought that self-directing speech is used to direct behaviour and has a central role in cognitive development.

Whereas in young children, self-directing speech is spoken aloud, in older children, and perhaps adults, this kind of speech is usually sub-vocal. Older children may think to themselves instead of talking to themselves. However, even in older children, this type of speech may become audible, especially if the child is faced with a challenging problem. School-aged children may vocalise when learning lists or trying to work out complex problems.

✔ PROGRESS CHECK

1 What are language pragmatics?
2 What is self-directing speech?
3 What is the link between self-directing speech and cognitive development?

SUMMARY OF LANGUAGE DEVELOPMENT

Table 3.1 summarises the information given in this chapter. The rate of development of language in children varies considerably, so the ages given are only approximate.

Table 3.1 A summary of language development, birth – 8 years

Age	Language development	Activities to promote language
Birth	Babies communicate by crying, moving and gazing. Parents and carers can identify babies' needs by differences in the cry.	Check babies' hearing as soon as possible after birth. Respond to cries promptly. Surround infant with language, use care-giving routines as opportunities for language development.
1–2 months	Babies begin to 'coo' (vowel sounds) when happy. They laugh and gurgle. They communicate by crying, smiling and eye contact. They can hold 'conversations' with parent or carer. They respond to adults by turn-taking and gazing into the adult's eyes.	A good, responsive, secure and stable relationship with parents and carers is needed. Key worker system important. Adult should use every opportunity to enter into 'conversations' with babies. Show you are pleased with them when they respond. Use songs and rhymes. Do not have the TV or radio on constantly in the background.
6 months	Babbling sounds appear, consisting of sounds made up of consonants and vowels. At first sounds do not always correspond to those heard in the language spoken around them.	Continue with the activities already stated. Include the baby in all family activities, especially family mealtimes. Talk to the child about everything you are doing.
9–12 months	Babies continue to babble, which begins to sound more like the language that they hear around them. The sounds not heard in their language are lost and the intonation becomes similar to that of the language they hear. Children who are deaf do not show these changes. Babbling may contain strings of sounds. Babies introduce gestures and facial expressions into their communications. They can wave 'bye-bye', respond to their name, understand *no* and may respond to a request, e.g. *look at the dog*.	Continue with previous activities. Obtain expert help if the baby's babbling doesn't change. Play games such as 'Pat-a-cake', finger games and 'wave bye-bye'. If you are the key worker of a child who is exposed to more than one language, learn some games and songs in the language the baby hears at home. Share books with the baby. Point things out to the child, give her the names of objects all around her.
12 months	First word appears which may not correspond to a known word that they have heard. Later babies will use their first word that corresponds to a word in the language they are learning. First words are only used in limited situations, e.g. *cat* may only refer to family cat.	Continue all of the above.
13 months	Babies can use words spontaneously in different contexts, i.e. *cat* now used for all cats. Toddlers use a mixture of babbling and words. They talk to themselves using 'jargon'. They use language to communicate. There is an increasing use of gesture.	Praise the child when she uses words correctly. Give the child instructions, e.g. *give me the ball*. Continue playing finger games, singing, using rhymes and stories. Introduce the child to more books especially ones which show everyday objects and events. Include books that reflect the child's culture, etc.

continued ▶

Table 3.1 *continued*

Age	Language development	Activities to promote language
14–19 months	The child's first 50 words (approx.) are learned slowly. After this there is an explosion in their vocabulary with a rapid increase in words learned. Most words are nouns at first. Children have conversations with adults. They enjoy books and singing. They can point to parts of their body, objects around them and can increasingly supply the correct word, although they may over-extend the use of a word, e.g. all animals may be called *doggie*. Single words can often represent whole sentences – holophrases.	Don't rush a child who is talking to you and maintain eye contact whilst speaking to her. Continue to name things around the child. Encourage the child to use her vocabulary by asking her to point to her head or arm, etc. When reading to her, ask her questions, e.g. *What's this?* or *Show me the duck.*
18– 30 months	Children start to put words together to form simple sentences. Telegraphic speech is used containing only the essential words, usually nouns, verbs and adjectives. No plurals or past tenses are used. Children can refer to themselves by name.	Encourage child to speak to other children and adults directly, but be ready to 'translate' if the message is unclear. Don't try to correct all the child's errors, negative attention may contribute to speech disorders. When a child uses a short, simple sentence expand the sentences in your reply. Speak slowly, using short sentences. Be a positive role model, don't use inappropriate language. Continue sharing books, songs, stories and rhymes with the child.
30 months–3 years	Children's sentences become increasingly complex. They can use the past tense, plurals and prepositions such as *on* and *in*. They make errors of over-regularisation, e.g. *sheeps* instead of *sheep*. Children may think faster than they can talk and may stumble over their words. They love to talk and ask questions constantly.	Encourage children to talk about their experiences. Don't rush children, let them see that you enjoy talking to them. Be patient and answer children's questions fully. Look for opportunities to increase children's vocabulary and explain the meaning of new words. Encourage children to talk on the telephone. Read to children and encourage them to join in by asking them to describe a picture or relate part of the story. Incorporate circle time into the routine of the nursery day. Sharing news and experiences encourages children to understand the function of language, develops the ability to take turns and encourages their listening skills.
3 years	Children will have a vocabulary of about 1,000 words. They love to sing and talk. 80 per cent of their speech is intelligible, although they may mispronounce *l, r, s* and *th*. They are able to use conjunctions such as *and* and *but*. They can talk about more than one idea at a time in a sentence and can use embedded clauses. They ask *why, when* and *how* questions and can talk about the future and the past. They can talk about, size, shape, colour and texture. They can tell a story from a picture and use different voices for different roles. They enjoy jokes and nonsense words.	Adults should show interest and appreciation of what is being said. Discuss children's drawings and paintings with them. Don't ask them what they have drawn but encourage them to tell you all about their picture. Avoid too many closed questions. Listen to children when they talk to you and bring them back to the subject if the conversation begins to drift. Give eye contact when children are talking to you and encourage children to look at you. Continue to answer all questions fully. Increase the number and type of books you use .
4 years	Children have a vocabulary of about 1,500 words. They talk in an adult fashion and are easy to understand. They ask lots of questions and are able to talk about ideas and experiences.	Continue using songs, stories and rhymes.
5–8 years	At 5 years children have a vocabulary of about 2,000 words. As they develop they use more complex and difficult forms of speech. They can understand the passive by about 6 years, but will not be able to use it until much later. Over-regularisation disappears and their vocabulary is increasing all the time. They become more aware of the functions of language and how to alter their speech according to whom they are speaking.	Ways to aid language development for older children are discussed in Chapter 4.

KEY TERMS

You need to know the meaning of the following words and phrases. Go back through the chapter to make sure you understand them:

babbling
contentives
cooing
expressive language
grammatical markers or inflections
holophrase
jargon
language pragmatics
pre-linguistic stage of language development
receptive language
reduplicated monosyllable
sound discrimination
stage one grammar
stage two grammar
telegraphic speech

FURTHER READING

Bee, H. (1995) *The Developing Child*, Longman
Gross, R. (1996) *The Science of Mind and Behaviour*, Hodder & Stoughton
   Both these books have good chapters on language development and would be suitable for students studying at levels three and four.

Listening and speaking

The key topics covered in this chapter are:

- Listening
- Speaking
- Listening and speaking to young children
- Developing listening and speaking skills in nurseries and schools.

The importance of children's oral and listening skills has been known for some time. It is essential to be aware of what is appropriate development in these areas as a deficit in these skills can be a predictor of later difficulties. In England and Wales, Speaking and Listening forms an integral part of the Early Years Curriculum for pre-school children and of the National Curriculum for children over the age of 5 years. Scotland and Northern Ireland have their own curriculum requirements. In seeking to enhance children's listening and speaking skills adults need to be aware of the role they play in this process. Adults are powerful role models, and if we are competent listeners and speakers and value these attributes, the children will do likewise.

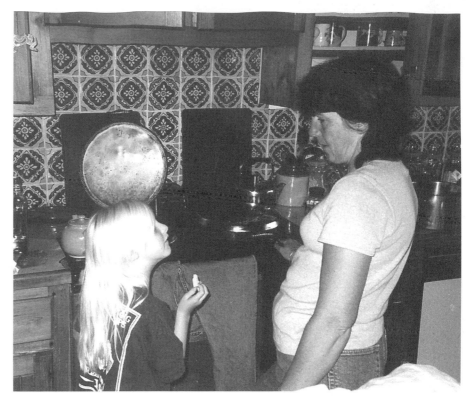

If adults are good listeners, children will learn to do likewise

LISTENING

What is listening?

You might have felt that you could go on making a very long list in response to the first exercise. Your list of reasons may have included to:

- hear what has been said
- find out information
- understand what others want to communicate to you
- know how best to help others
- be part of a group
- enjoy music and poetry
- enjoy sounds in nature
- warn of danger

and many others.

A simple definition of listening would be *to hear the sounds in our environment using our sense of hearing*. The earliest people probably had a much more acute sense of hearing than we have, finely tuned for survival. We are now living in an environment where we have to cope with a myriad of different sounds, as well as a considerable amount of noise pollution. Our hearing skills have evolved to enable us to cope with a plethora of background noise, particularly in urban areas, and the skills we particularly need to develop are to be able to listen selectively and concentrate on what immediately needs our attention. Children need to develop these skills and the adults who care for them have to be aware that such development requires to be nurtured.

Children living in urban areas may have to cope with a myriad of background sounds

An acute awareness of sounds is not much use unless we understand their meaning. It is the *understanding* of the sounds and gestures of spoken language that makes communication between people possible. In other words, it is the understanding of the listener that completes a communicative act. We all know that unless the person we are talking to listens to us with a desire to understand we can talk for ever and still not communicate. Hearing is a passive act – we usually hear whether we want to or not, but listening is an active process which involves processing the meaning of the words we hear in order to understand them.

It has been estimated that only 10 per cent of our communication is represented by the selection of words we use; a further 30 per cent by what is heard by the listener and the remaining 60 per cent by our body language. The skill of listening is not effective unless there is a sincere desire to understand what is being said. If we are to develop this skill in ourselves and particularly in the children we care for, we need to be aware that listening involves all of the following:

- listening with our ears and carefully differentiating between sounds
- understanding the meaning of the words used
- using our eyes to see and understand the body language being used
- tuning into the use of paralanguage
- intuitive understanding

THINK ABOUT IT

Think of a conversation you have had recently with someone with whom you particularly wanted to communicate. Did you get your points across to the other person? Was this because they:

- heard the words you actually spoke?
- had encouraging body language that made communication easy for you?
- wanted badly to know what you had to say?
- understood what you wanted them to know?
- had well developed listening skills?
- found it easy to agree with what you had to say?

You might have decided that you were able to communicate effectively because a combination of the above applied.

DEFINITIONS

contextual understanding the choice of words, or the body language used, may depend on the situation

cultural understanding the language or culture of the speaker or listener may influence what is said or heard

- listening for feeling and meaning

- **contextual understanding** – the choice of words and the body language used depends on the situation

- **cultural understanding** – the choice of language by a speaker who is using their second or subsequent language may alter meaning and body language and paralanguage may also have different meanings in different cultural groups

- clearing our minds, when appropriate, of assumptions we may have about the speakers themselves or their intending meanings. We need also to be aware that such assumptions may sometimes help our understanding.

Listening is therefore an art, a skill, a discipline and an essential attribute which needs to be continually developed if we are to be truly effective communicators ourselves and models of good communication for our children. The best ways of enhancing listening skills have formed part of the training of business and industrial executives for many years. Though such training is often good in nursery nurse or teacher training, it is occasionally ignored or treated as a subsidiary skill. All child-care practitioners have the responsibility of being good models of effective listening to the children in their care. They need to work as team members which necessitates the ability to listen and understand. They are also partners with parents in the care and education of their children and this also requires effective listening skills.

Being partners with parents/carers in the care and education of their children requires effective listening skills

CASE STUDY

Miriam

Miriam had trained as a nursery nurse and had spent five years working with children in a large, busy nursery. She had recently completed her Advanced Diploma in Childcare and Education and was delighted to find that she had been offered a job in a day-care centre. She was deeply committed to quality care for children and knew that staff members had to feel valued as members of a team if they were to provide this. She fully accepted that parents/carers had to be partners with nursery staff in their children's care and education.

Soon Miriam began to find that she was having problems with both staff members and parents which, when analysed, seemed to be the result of inadequate communication. When talking to them she seemed to possess all the skills that might be expected. When someone talked to her she generally gave the impression that she really cared about what was said and listened carefully. She would make good eye contact, nod her head and now and then make some appropriate small response like 'I see'. The problem was that Miriam was giving the outward appearance of listening but was not really doing so. During a management training course, which contained a module on effective communication, Miriam's problem was pointed out to her. She took this very seriously and immediately started to work on her listening techniques. To her relief and surprise she found that many minor problems of communication disappeared within weeks.

1 Why was Miriam having problems communicating with staff members and parents?

2 Why would the management training course have been useful to Miriam before she started the job?

3 Why did her efforts to improve her listening skills improve staff and parent relationships?

Different ways of listening

Communication (using speech) is not just about talking – it is about listening too. We are aware that no matter how well a speaker presents his or her subject or a conversationalist uses his or her skill, effective communication also depends on the listener. Information can be sent by a speaker but it must be received and accepted by an active listener. Different situations may demand different types of listening, but it is important for our **interpersonal skills** that we know the type of listening we do. Reflecting on how we listen improves our skills and enhances communication.

Some of the less effective ways of listening to others include:

● *Basic interest* We often develop this type of listening to cope with everyday

DEFINITION

interpersonal skills   the skill of interacting in a reciprocal way between two people

conversations (and the radio and television). We pick up enough of what has been said and show enough interest to keep the other person talking reasonably comfortably. We often forget much of what has been said unless there is some traumatic reason to force recall. Child-care practitioners who are unable to throw themselves into the real work of being with children and meeting their language and communication needs will often listen like this.

- *Rehearsing* We give the impression we are listening but our whole attention is on designing and preparing our next comment. We are thinking about what to say next and how it will serve our own needs and perhaps the effect it will have on the speaker. This can sometimes happen with team meetings, especially with inexperienced staff. Taken to extremes this could result in two monologues and no communication.

- *Judging* It is very hard to really listen with interest and understanding to someone we may prejudge as being incompetent or uninformed. We may hear their words and even tune into their emotion, but we may have conditioned ourselves to pay little attention to them. It is a basic rule of listening not to make judgements until you have listened to the content of the message. This type of listening can happen when child care practitioners do not sufficiently value parental contributions.

- *Own experience viewpoint* We listen but each item that is communicated is referred back to our own experience. We can't wait for the speaker to stop so that we can launch forth on what happened to us.

- *Advising/giving information* We listen enough to pick up the gist of what is being said, but we spend our time searching for the right advice or information to give. The communicator often does not get a chance to tell you what is most important. Research into adult–child conversations in nurseries has sometimes shown that adults adopt this mode when talking to young children. They are anxious to give the children new vocabulary, ideas and information. They forget to listen and the children are deprived of opportunities to communicate and observe good listening skills in adults.

- *Changing the subject* Poor listeners will often change the subject because they have got tired of listening.

- *Automatic responses* Adults dealing with a large number of children may sometimes respond in this way, responding with a word like 'Super!' to a child's attempt to say something about their painting.

- *Supportive/placating* We listen enough to get the drift of a communication but we are not really involved in helping the person, but in being liked ourselves. So we make responses like 'Yes, of course...', 'I know', 'Absolutely...'.

- *Day dreaming* When we daydream we pretend to listen but we really only pretend to listen while we drift off into our interior fantasies. Instead of disciplining ourselves to truly listen we think of more entertaining subjects.

Inexperienced staff will sometimes rehearse rather than listen at team meetings

THINK ABOUT IT

Think of a conversation you have had with a person, whom on reflection, you feel may have been listening to you in one or several of the above ways. How did you feel? Did you finish telling that person what you set out to tell him/her when you started the conversation? Would you seek that person out if you had a problem you wanted to discuss?

We may be initially horrified to think that we would use some or all of the above methods of listening. However, one of the first steps in improving any skill is to know what we can stop doing in order to perform better. It is also essential that we are aware of the need always to have respect for any speaker and their communication. In addition, knowing the effects of poor listening skills on others should help us to strive to develop better and more effective listening skills ourselves.

Listening effectively to others (and this includes children) is the most powerful method of communication. When someone is an effective listener many communication problems disappear. Good listeners listen with their ears, eyes, brain and intuition. Insights are gained into the intellectual, perceptual and emotional world of the speaker. The capacity of a person (or child) to communicate effectively – structuring their ideas and choosing the right vocabulary – is enhanced if they are aware that they are being carefully listened to.

Effective listening involves:

- paying attention only to what the speaker has to communicate – concerns which the listener may have are temporarily suspended

- paying attention to the words being used – the words a speaker selects to convey information are important and a particular selection of words can sometimes convey subtle meanings

- maintaining appropriate eye contact and body positioning – this makes it easier for the person speaking to us to communicate

- using eyes as well as understanding to pick up communication cues from the speaker's body language

- paying attention to vocal paralanguage – listening to the tone of voice used can help us to understand a communication

- using intuitive understanding of what is being said

- encouraging the speaker appropriately by nodding, smiling, saying 'Yes', 'I understand', etc.
- asking for clarification of points you may not understand – this is important in helping a listener to have a clearer understanding of what is being said and it may also encourage a speaker
- **paraphrasing** – it may help when there is a natural break in the conversation to briefly restate in your own words what you have heard
- being able to give immediate, honest and supportive feedback.

If you are interrupted by a matter that urgently needs your attention it is a good idea to apologise to the speaker and remember to return to the subject as soon as appropriate. If children, in particular, are treated in this way, they will feel that their communication is valued in addition to learning courtesy.

DEFINITION
paraphrase   using other words in an attempt to make the meaning of what has been said easier to understand

GOOD PRACTICE

- Attendance at listening skills workshops should be encouraged as part of staff training. These may be included as in-service training and/or where possible staff should be encouraged to attend short courses on developing listening skills.
- All staff in nurseries and schools should aim to be effective listeners. It is particularly important for senior staff members to have good listening skills as they are role models for all staff, parents and children.
- What is listened to is important. Sometimes you may have to tell somebody that you do not wish to listen to what they want to say. It may be important not to listen to gossip or you may make a decision not to listen to somebody's communication because you do not feel it is appropriate for you to listen and that what is being communicated requires more specialist help, for example, from a counsellor or senior staff member.
- Be aware that you should avoid taking on the role of counsellor unless you have had specialised training in counselling.
- From time to time, assess your personal listening skills using, as a guide, the list of effective listening skills on these pages. It is useful to do this just after you have had a meeting with a parent/carer or another team member to discuss an important issue.
- Be aware that you cannot be a perfect listener all the time. It may sometimes be necessary to tell somebody that you found it hard to listen because of tiredness or other distractions and that you want them to repeat the communication.

The value of listening

If we listen well we understand more. Relationships with those with whom we live or work are very important and knowing that someone is willing to listen with respect makes communication easier. When listened to by others, individuals tend to listen to themselves more and to evaluate and clarify their own thoughts and feelings. The value of listening well cannot be dealt with adequately in a short section of a book but the following list may be considered as some of the benefits of good listening:

- Children's learning skills are enhanced if they learn to become good listeners.
- We become role models of good listening for children and for others.

- We have better understanding of material presented in meetings, conversations and lectures.

- There are fewer misunderstandings and hurt feelings, leading to the development of good relationships.

- It stops us being egocentric in our approach to the world. We develop the understanding that everyone has a valid message to impart, even the inarticulate and those who differ from us politically, culturally and in other ways.

- Listening to others with interest is more intellectually stimulating and enjoyable.

- We become better problem-solvers.

- Good listeners are better and more professional members of our work team.

✔ PROGRESS CHECK

1 In addition to hearing the sounds of spoken language, what else is essential for good communication?

2 List four features which are involved in good listening.

3 What might we be doing, when listening, which would prevent us from understanding what another person is communicating?

4 How might being listened to well help us as speakers?

5 List six of the features of good listening.

6 Name four of the benefits of good listening.

SPEAKING

The use of speech is an integral part of human communication. It is generally believed that children all over the world start putting words together at approximately the same age. The development of their abilities to use speech follow very similar paths.

The development of human speech

The use of sound to send messages is not a unique human skill as it is used in the animal world as well. When animals send sounds, however, there is usually a strong recognisable link between the sound and the message it wishes to convey. A cat, for example, in addition to making a sound which indicates attack will also arch its back, spit and appear ready to pounce. The big difference between animals and humans is that, in addition to having a much wider range of sounds, the sound system used by humans is arbitrary (i.e. it is random). Human words are not tied to the sound of the thing named. For example, there is no connection between the word *camel* and the animal it symbolises. There are exceptions, known as **onomatopoeia**, such as *quack quack* and *bang*, where the sound of the word represents its meaning.

Historical linguists feel that humans probably acquired their sound signalling systems fairly late in their evolution. This seems true because all the organs used in speech have some more basic function – teeth, lips and tongue are used for eating; the lungs are used for breathing; the vocal cords were used primarily for closing off the lungs in order to make the rib cage rigid for actions requiring extra effort. We still use such actions today for weightlifting and childbirth.

One of the differences between animal and human sound systems is that animals seem to be born with their sound systems already functioning. Human babies take some time to develop the physical skills necessary to speak and even when these have been developed there is still a long learning process, requiring cultural input, before acquisition of language is complete. The carefully documented, rare cases of children brought up by animals without human contact – known as feral children – show how necessary this cultural input is, as these children could only make a limited number of sounds similar to those heard in the wild. Human beings are probably born with an innate predisposition towards language (see page 29), but this can be activated only by exposure to it.

Human babies take some time to develop the physical skills necessary to speak

The uses of speech

An inability to use speech adequately can affect someone's status in their group, at school or in society. Its importance in education and in general understanding about the world becomes very obvious even when children are in nursery school. The child who has an age-appropriate command of speech will find it much easier to get on socially and emotionally as well as intellectually.

Children will need to begin to develop speaking skills, which as adults they will use for many purposes – conversations, giving directions, asking for and giving information, giving presentations, making speeches, etc. There are many ways of encouraging children to develop good speaking skills. These include:

DO THIS!

If you are working in a nursery or school, spend some time reflecting on how the staff use spoken language. Is it ever discussed in team meetings? Would it be helpful if it was? You may wish to discuss the answers to these questions with your study group if you are part of one.

- speaking in as clear a voice as possible. We need to develop an awareness of the appropriate pronunciation of words. We should value whatever accent we may happen to have as part of the rich fabric of the environment and not consider that it might be inferior to any other accent. The use of any accent does not hinder appropriate pronunciation. Derogatory imitation of accents is never acceptable no matter how humorously done

- having a knowledge of word order and the correct structure of sentences

- paying some attention to voice dynamics – volume, pace, pause and pitch are all important. An awareness of this can be developed by listening to ourselves on a tape recorder. These can be as important as the words used in our communication. A loud strident voice may convey the message in the words used, but it may also convey perhaps the desire to dominate or the insecurity of the speaker

- being aware that words alone do not necessarily convey all of the meaning and that body language is a powerful conveyer of information. Paying attention to body positioning and eye contact will encourage us to speak with more confidence

- being able to reflect on the use of speech. We get better at talking partly because we reflect on what we say ourselves and on the speech of others. Telling someone that they spoke clearly when giving information at a meeting is very encouraging and produces even better speech.

DEFINITION

Standard English   the English which has the highest status in the English-speaking world and which is based on the speech and writing of educated speakers

The expectation in schools in England and Wales is that pupils should be able to speak, read and write using **Standard English**. This is one of the requirements of the National Curriculum which states that 'Pupils should be introduced with appropriate sensitivity to the importance of Standard English.' It follows that if we are working with children we should also be using Standard English ourselves. This idea is controversial.

The thinking which underpins this expectation is that if everyone has access to it, Standard English will create equality in society. However, many educationists feel that in every child there are issues of identity involved which are far more important than how spoken language sounds or is

Issues of identity can be far more important than how language sounds

DEFINITION

dialect a form of language spoken in a particular region or by members of a particular group or class of people, distinguished by the vocabulary (words used), grammar, pronunciation (accent) and use of idiom; also referred to as speech varieties

structured. Standard English is one more **dialect** among many and the fact that it is considered correct is more to do with its status as being the dialect used by the educated or wealthier classes. Linguists are more concerned with semantic appropriateness, knowing that language is constantly evolving and changing. There is no reason why Standard English cannot be used by anyone as their second or third language as long as their community dialect or other language is not seen as inferior.

✔ PROGRESS CHECK

1 What are the differences between animal and human sound systems?

2 What is the basic function of speech?

3 In your own words describe four different ways in which speech is used.

4 Explain what Standard English is.

5 Do we need to have a particular accent in order to speak well?

LISTENING AND SPEAKING WITH YOUNG CHILDREN

Children as speakers and listeners

As we have already seen, spoken language and the ability to listen to it is an important aspect of all communication. Children develop these skills just as they do any others, but the degree to which these skills are encouraged and nurtured will have a profound effect on their educational, social and emotional success. It has always been assumed that children who listened well learned better, but the importance of children's oral skills has also been known for some time. Children vary in the rate at which they acquire the ability to use oral language. A perceived lack in this area can be a predictor of later difficulties. Most children have no problem, but when children enter school with only a rudimentary vocabulary and speech patterns that are not age-appropriate, their speech and language skills need to be closely monitored. It is now well established that language and literacy development is about speaking and listening as well as about reading and writing.

DEFINITION

articulate to produce speech sounds in the mouth and throat

GOOD PRACTICE

- Be a good role model of speaking and listening. Children consciously and unconsciously absorb the habits and practices of the social group to which they belong.
- Be aware of the importance of developing speaking and listening in the children in your care.
- Be aware that children's communication deserves the same respect as adults. Children need to be listened to and responded to in ways that are age-appropriate. Pre-school children can often understand more than they can **articulate**.

Listening and responding to children does not mean that they should be allowed to constantly interrupt and demand attention. This is perhaps less likely to happen if they are used to being listened to.

- Regularly review how carefully you listen to the children in your care. Consider if there are factors that make listening difficult for you. Are there skills or habits you could develop to make listening easier?

Parents/carers are their children's first educators. They have the opportunity to encourage good speaking and listening skills in their children from the beginning. All adults, whether child-care practitioners or not, can learn from the many parents who communicate well with their children.

- give children opportunities to talk and listen
- use language that is appropriate to the children's level
- help children to look and listen at the same time by gesturing and pointing when giving directions – this helps understanding as well as maintaining interest
- listen carefully and show interest in what the children have to say
- practise the skill of talking *with* children, not at them
- say what they mean and mean what they say – a child should not be teased unless the adult is quite sure that the child understands that it is teasing and knows how to handle it
- sing to children – songs, rhymes and poetry aid children in absorbing the sounds, rhythm and flow of language
- play different types of music and encourage quiet listening – a different type of music could be played each day at lunch time. As the children get older there can be discussions on which type of music the child prefers
- play rhyming and word games with them
- when children begin to understand spoken language, give one-step directions, for example *Bring me your shoe*
- later, give two-step directions, for example, *Pick up that car and put it into your toy box*
- later still, give three-step directions, such as *Put your shoes on, get your coat and get into the car*, to build listening and memory skills – but children need to be able to cope with two-step directions first
- expect children to listen to them – discourage them from walking away when they are being talked to
- avoid raising their voice or shouting at children except in an emergency when a child needs to be stopped doing something dangerous – children who are constantly shouted at tend to not listen to ordinary voice tone
- help children to be aware of sounds in their environment both inside and outside
- describe sounds using sound language like *high*, *low*, *loud* and *faraway*
- talk about sounds with children – discussions on the sounds that animals make often provides an opportunity to do this
- read stories and poems.

You can probably think of many other ways in which adults can help children to be competent listeners and speakers.

Read stories and poems to children

✔ PROGRESS CHECK

1 What should happen when children enter school with poorly-developed speaking skills?
2 Why do adults need to be good role models of speaking and listening for young children?
3 List three things which adults need to be aware of in order to help young children to be effective speakers and listeners.
4 Name four things which adults can do to help children to develop their speaking and listening skills.

DEVELOPING LISTENING AND SPEAKING SKILLS IN NURSERIES AND SCHOOLS

Children in pre-school settings

The previous section dealt with the many ways that all adults can nurture the speaking and listening development of the children in their care. The UK government has issued guidelines for child-care practitioners and teachers in England and Wales aimed at incorporating speaking and listening skills into nursery and school curricula.

The Early Years curriculum is designed to guide practitioners in such a way that when children enter compulsory schooling it is expected that they can:

- recount events or experiences
- ask questions to find out information and be able to listen to the answers
- make up their own story and tell it
- make up a story with detail and tell it to a small group.

Children need to be provided with a wide range of materials and experiences which encourage the development of these skills. They need to be able to understand how to speak and listen in:

- activity-based sharing situations
- discussions
- news telling
- descriptions
- narrative
- pair work and team work
- inquiry
- conversation
- a range of social settings
- large and small groups.

Pair work helps children to develop speaking skills

Much of what has been said in the previous sections about the ways in which adults can develop and encourage children's speaking and listening skills applies to children in nurseries. Pre-school settings are run by trained practitioners who know the value of having a structured approach to all children's learning needs. They also know the value of both long- and short-term planning to meet these needs, as well as the need for flexibility. Spontaneous happenings both indoors and outside provide many opportunities for enjoyably extending children's speaking and listening skills.

Practitioners also need to be aware that pre-school children are often much less able to modify their messages to ensure that their listeners understand. Even when listeners state their difficulty, young children often have problems in responding appropriately. Unlike older children, who might understand that they could do something about being understood, young children often blame the listener and switch off. This is not to suggest, however, that young children are always insensitive to listener needs; they just have more difficulty understanding them and need to be helped in the course of their activities to be aware of this aspect of human communication and respond to it.

The work of a group of psychologists at the University of Edinburgh in the 1970s (reported by one of them, Margaret Donaldson, in 1978) showed that adults can be **egocentric** in their approach to young children – they are sometimes unable or unwilling to look at something from a child's perspective. They assume that because a child cannot understand something or express an idea it is because the child is not intellectually or linguistically mature. Young children should be encouraged and supported in their efforts to make themselves understood. They need to be listened to carefully, supplied with appropriate vocabulary and difficulties in understanding discussed.

GOOD PRACTICE

- Children should be given the opportunity to engage in conversations as well as listening to instructions and explanations.
- Provide children with a wide variety of activities both indoors and outside, as well as outings, visits from parents and members of the community and celebrations. In this way both children and adults have a lot to talk about.
- Ensure that children have many opportunities to develop their vocabularies.
- Talk about, and give them opportunities to listen to other languages, dialects and accents. Take care to avoid bias and stereotypical attitudes. You may first need to examine your own feelings.
- Provide opportunities for children to listen to sounds other than speech – music, sounds in nature (weather, animals), sound of machines, etc.
- Describe sounds to children and get them to describe a particular sound. They will need to be familiar with words such as high, low, soft, hard, grating, soothing, etc.
- Use all areas of the curriculum to develop speaking and listening skills. When planning, think about how speaking and listening can be specifically incorporated into activities.
- Play listening games on a regular basis.
- Ensure that children are read to as much as possible. Concentrating on adult story reading skills is probably one of the best ways to encourage children's listening skills. Stories develop children's vocabularies and give them confidence when speaking.
- Be aware of the need to provide time and opportunity to meet the needs of individual children. It could be easy to go though a day or even a week without having much conversation with quiet and shy children.
- Ensure that all children listen to adults or children who speak to them. Adults should expect to be listened to. Creating this ethos in a nursery not only makes managing a large group of children easier, but it also ensures a safer environment. Children learn that 'switching off' when someone speaks is not the way to behave.
- Be a good adult role model. Be careful not to 'switch off' yourself when the children are talking. If you listen carefully to children and make an effort to understand what they want to communicate, children will tend to do likewise.

DO THIS!

Plan in detail a listening activity for a group of three 4-year-olds. List the main aims of the activity.

Later carry it out and write an evaluation. You can do this by discussing whether each of your aims was met. Consider whether you would repeat the same activity in the same way on another occasion.

You can probably think of other ways to encourage children's speaking and listening. The nursery environment should be geared to help children develop these skills by having quiet areas, areas where noise can be made, areas where sounds can be explored, reading areas and places where spontaneous conversations can happen. A specific listening area where children can listen to music, stories and poems on tape is valuable. Projects on sound or accents and dialects can be interesting for both children and adults. Tape recording and listening to their own voices and those of their friends is also a useful activity. A welcoming atmosphere will also ensure that parents/carers feel they can linger and have a conversation with a member of staff. If children are allowed to listen in and contribute to these conversations this can be as valuable as starting straight into the planned activities for the day.

Children 5–8 years

For children in this age group in England and Wales, the National Curriculum sets out the knowledge, understanding and skills to be taught in nine different subject areas. For Speaking and Listening, the Programme of Study intends that children in this age range should be given opportunities to talk for a range of purposes, including:

- to tell stories, both factual and from their imaginations; play imaginatively and take part in drama; read and listen to nursery rhymes and poetry, learn some by heart; read aloud
- to be able to explore, develop and clarify ideas; predict outcomes and discuss possibilities
- to describe events, observations and experiences; make simple, clear explanations of choices and give reasons for opinions and actions

Children should also be given the opportunity to consider how talk is influenced by the purpose and by the intended audience. They should be able to work in groups of different sizes, and be able to talk and present work to different audiences, including friends, the class, the teacher and other adults in the school.

Children should be able to listen carefully and to show their understanding of what they see and hear by making relevant comments. They should be encouraged to remember specific points that interest them, and to listen to the reactions of others.

Children should be encouraged to participate in drama activities, improvisation and performances of various kinds as well as respond to drama they have watched.

In order to be able to do the above, children should be taught the importance of:

- using language that is clear and fluent
- speaking with confidence
- choosing the correct words to express what they want to say
- distinguishing between relevant and irrelevant detail when giving explanations, descriptions or narratives
- using the conventions of discussion and conversation, i.e. structuring their talk in ways that are clear and understandable and taking turns.

In the delivery of the curriculum in Language and Literacy, Mathematics, Science and any other subject area, there are opportunities for listening to instructions, asking questions, taking part in conversations, small and large group discussions and formal presentations. Planning in these and any other area must include opportunities for children to:

- have initial informal discussions
- select and prioritise possibilities
- prepare for investigations
- get information from each other and from adults
- plan written work
- reflect on what has been done so far

- talk about what they have achieved
- have small group and/or whole-class presentations.

Progress in oral skills normally develops from straightforward responses to direct questions to child-initiated discussion. Children advance from having informal discussions with peers or teachers to being able to present information to the whole class. As a project or theme develops, their general and specialist vocabularies increase.

Influence on a child's life

All learning, both formal and informal, in the Early Years, is vitally important for children's later educational progress. But the foundations laid by the development of the best speaking and listening skills possible have the power to enhance an individual's whole life. If we work tirelessly at developing these skills in the children in our care, not only will they benefit, but we as adults will also benefit because we will have had to reflect on how we speak and listen ourselves.

> 'The world is full of words. There are so many talking all the time, loudly, quietly, in rooms, on streets, on TV, on radio, in the paper, in books. The noise of words keeps what we call the world there for us. We take each other's sounds and make patterns, predictions, benedictions and blasphemies. Each day, our tribe of language holds what we call the "world" together. Yet the uttering of the word reveals how each of us relentlessly creates. Everyone is an artist. Each person brings sound out of silence and coaxes the invisible to become visible.'
>
> (O'Donoghue, J. (1997) *Anam Cara*, Bantam Press)

 **PROGRESS CHECK**

1 What language skills are children expected to have when they enter compulsory education?

2 What might be the reaction of a 3-year-old child who feels that what they have just said might not be understood by the listener?

3 List four ways that children can be helped to become good speakers and listeners.

4 List five skills which children aged 5–8 might need to acquire.

FURTHER READING

Donaldson, M. (1978) *Children's Minds*, Fontana
  This book explains how adults can often misunderstand children. It highlights the need for adults to think carefully about the language they use when they are talking to children.
Yates, I. (1998) *Language and Literacy*, Scholastic
  This would be helpful to increase understanding of the importance of listening and speaking in the development of children's language and literacy.

KEY TERMS

You need to know the meaning of the following words and phrases. Go back through the chapter to make sure you understand them:

articulate
contextual understanding
cultural understanding
dialect
historical linguist
interpersonal skills
onomatopoeia
paraphrase
Standard English

The development of reading

The key topics covered in this chapter are:

- What is reading?
- Theoretical approaches to reading
- Laying the foundations for reading in the under-3s
- Developing early literacy skills in the 3–5s
- Developing reading skills in the 5–7s (school age).

The ability to read is one of the most important skills that a child needs to aquire because it is the key to so many other areas of learning. In the past, encouraging reading skills was seen to be the job of the nursery or infant teacher. Now it is recognised that all child-care practitioners have a role to play, as do parents. This chapter is designed to explain some of the principles behind learning to read and to give practical suggestions to encourage the development of reading skills.

WHAT IS READING?

Reading: a complex process

DEFINITION

reading understanding the meaning of written or printed words or symbols, or speaking such words aloud

Most of us would agree with the following definition from the *Oxford Guide to the English Language*, that **reading** is 'understanding the meaning of written or printed words or symbols, or speaking such words aloud'.

Consider the following scenario. A mother brings her daughter aged 3½ to nursery for the first time and proudly tells the nursery nurse that the child can read. What does this mean? The child may be able to read fluently but it is more likely that the child knows a few letters, can identify a few words or may even recognise one or two familiar phrases.

Learning to read is not like learning to tie a shoe lace. When a child learns to tie a shoe lace there is a period when she learns the various movements that she has to do to tie the lace and eventually she becomes proficient. Once the skill is learned the process is complete. With reading, learning is different. There is never a time when it is possible to say that an adult or child has learned everything there is to know about reading. Whatever your age and however proficient your reading skills, there are always areas where your skills could be improved. For instance, you may find that some books are easy to read, whilst others, such as textbooks, are more of a challenge.

Before you can teach a child to read, you need to have a good understanding of what reading is for. Only then can you identify the skills, competencies and understanding that children need to become efficient readers.

What reading is used for

In the exercise above, you were probably able to identify that you need to be able to read to do your job, to complete a course, to find out information and read instructions. See how much of the following you thought of.

Personal uses of reading
These include reading :

- for enjoyment/relaxation, seeking information about hobbies
- to children
- letters from friends
- business letters about household administration
- instructions manuals
- to find information, bus timetables and financial material
- signs when driving or using public transport
- to gain more knowledge, to be able to make informed choices and be in control of one's life.

THINK ABOUT IT

Write down all the reasons why you need to be able to read.

Reading for information

Reading at school or workplace

This includes reading:

- books and other texts to get information that gives access to all curriculum areas
- at an advanced level where one has to extract ideas, analyse them, compare and contrast different points of view
- and understanding reports, memos, policy documents, planning documents and letters
- instructions and safety information.

The importance of reading for society

Reading is important because:

- if adults are unable to read they often cannot find work, or only get low-paid employment
- the inability to read can lead to poverty and social exclusion
- the economy suffers if workers do not have the advanced skills of flexible and critical reading that are needed in a fast changing, complex society.

Once it has been defined what reading is for, educators can then devise curricula that are designed to give children and young people the skills they will need in future life. Each child will need to be helped to discover their own reasons for wanting to read and to see that the ability to read is of great personal benefit to them.

DO THIS!

Ask ten adults who you know to describe how they learned to read. If possible include someone who learned to read in a different country. Ask them:

- if they can remember any reading schemes that were used
- whether they were taught the sounds of the alphabet (phonics) or to learn whole words at a time? Some adults may remember being taught ITA, where text was written slightly different from ordinary English in an effort to make reading easier
- about any feelings or emotions they had about learning to read. Did they feel excitement or frustration? Did they feel a sense of achievement or were there problems?

If you are doing this exercise in a classroom situation, it will be interesting to compare your findings with those of other students.

✔ PROGRESS CHECK

1 Write your own definition of reading.
2 Why is learning to read different from learning to tie a shoe lace?
3 Give two of the uses for reading in the home.
4 Give two uses of reading outside the home.

THEORETICAL APPROACHES TO READING

How did you learn to read? Many of us can't really remember – it's something we always seem to have been able to do.

Over the years there have been many approaches to the teaching of reading. The method used at any time always reflects the models (or ways of thinking) about the processes involved in reading that are currently fashionable. Ann Browne (1998) has identified three basic models:

- the bottom-up model
- the top-down model
- the interactive model.

The bottom-up model

Reading is seen as a process where the text is decoded by matching the letter shape to a sound and building up the sound of a word. The words are then put together to form sentences. It follows from this that when teaching reading one starts by teaching the sound that goes with the printed symbol. In some methods the basic unit of language used is the word, rather than the letter.

The bottom-up model

The top-down model

In this model it is suggested that readers predict the meaning of a text from what they already know about the structure and meaning of language. They use their knowledge about the world, their knowledge about the structure of stories and visual cues from pictures to help them get the meaning from text. Only after they have a good idea about what the text is will they use skills of letter and word recognition.

The interactive model

This model puts the two other approaches together. Readers assume that a text is meaningful and will predict the meaning by using their knowledge about the subject matter, sentence construction and what they already know about written material. At the same time they will use what they know about sounds, letters and words to help understand the text. As children are exposed to more and more reading material they begin to recognise more words and are able to concentrate more on the meaning of the text.

Teaching methods

Many methods have been tried in an effort to find the 'best' way to teach children to read. Each method has had enthusiastic support at one time or another. In many cases the success or failure of any particular method lies in the skill and energy of the teachers involved, rather than in the actual method itself. In the classroom, although a particular method may dominate, many teachers use a variety of strategies. In 1975 the Bullock Report (a government report on the teaching of language in schools) stated that 'there is no one method, medium or approach, device or philosophy that holds the key to the process of learning to read'. This statement is still true today and you need to bear it in mind when you read the following section.

Each theoretical model, described previously, gives rise to different teaching methods. The bottom-up model is the basis for methods that introduce children to letters, words or sentences first. These include:

- the alphabetic method
- the phonic method
- the word method
- the sentence method.

The top-down model underpins the real books method.

The alphabetic method

In this method children are taught, first of all, to recognise the shape of individual letters of the alphabet and to name them. It is assumed that this will help them recognise and pronounce words. The method involves constant repetition of the letter names (for example, *dee-oe-gee* for *dog*). The main emphasis is on the recognition of new words rather than the meaning of the words. This is an old-fashioned method and is rarely used.

The phonic method

In this method the *sounds* of letters (or combinations of letters) are substituted for the letter names. Originally the sounds of individual letters were taught. This caused some confusion in children because letter sounds are never produced singly, but always together with other letter sounds in words. The position of the letter within a word often determines the sound of the letter. Also, if individual letters are sounded out there is a tendency for the child to add sounds so that *bat* may end up sounding like *barter*. Later there was more emphasis on teaching the sounds of letter combinations. One great difficulty with this method is that in English, one symbol (letter) can represent many sounds, for instance, the *a* sound in *car* and *cat*. One way around this was devised by Pitman in 1961 who introduced the Initial Teaching Alphabet, a modified alphabet where one symbol only had one sound. This was a popular method of teaching reading for a time, but has fallen into disuse.

The phonic method has returned to popularity in schools today. Research has indicated that the method is effective and schools are encouraged to introduce elements of phonic teaching in an effort to raise standards of literacy.

The word method

This is known as the whole-word approach or the look-and-say method. Children are taught to recognise words by their shape. It was thought that if you taught the child to recognise whole words, then the initial reading process would be speeded up and the child would find learning to read more satisfying.

In the whole-word method the child is taught to associate the word with the picture that the word stands for. In the same way, familiar objects around the classroom are labelled. The look-and-say method is similar, but does not rely on the association of word and picture so words other than nouns can be introduced. Words are written on cards and repeatedly shown to children until they are learned. Some reading schemes start with the child being taught a basic vocabulary of 20 words before being introduced to them in books.

The sentence method

In this method children are introduced to whole sentences, rather than words, in the beginning stages of learning to read. Reading material is based on children's interests and spoken vocabulary. For instance, children discuss their drawings with the teacher who then writes a sentence about it underneath the picture, using the children's words. Sometimes whole books are made in this way.

The real books method

The underlying theory behind this method is that children do not need to be taught how to decode text at the letter, word or sentence level because they learn to recognise words in the same way that they recognise other familiar objects in their environment. Instead of using reading schemes, children were encouraged to read books that interested them and contained 'real stories'. Reading was integrated throughout the curriculum so that the child was surrounded by opportunities to learn to recognise words. In this method the child is helped to extract meaning from the text by visual cues and by applying knowledge that they already have about stories and the structure of language.

There have been criticisms about this approach. Some children, with committed and enthusiastic teachers, developed good reading skills using this method. However most children need to be actively taught the basic skills of reading, and it is not recommended that this method is used on its own as a way of helping children learn to read.

The interactive approach

Research has indicated that methods of teaching based on the bottom-up model and the top-down model are not ideal. According to Ann Browne (1998), 'teaching children skills without giving them the information about their role as readers and why the process is important may result in the acquisition of knowledge that is not applied'. She also considers that introducing children to reading using a top-down model, without giving the children the skills they need to recognise what is written, is putting some children at a disadvantage. Browne proposes an approach that puts together the elements from both models. In this approach children are exposed to reading material that is relevant and has meaning to them and can demonstrate to them the processes and purposes or reading. But at the same time they are taught the skills that they need to make sense of print. In this way children will be given a wide range of strategies that they can use.

In reality, few teachers ever use one method of teaching children to read. In most classrooms a variety of methods have always been used, although one style may predominate.

✔ PROGRESS CHECK

1 Describe the three theoretical models of reading.

2 Give one method of teaching reading that relates to the top-down model.

3 Give one method of teaching reading that relates to the bottom-up model.

4 Describe the interactive approach.

LAYING THE FOUNDATIONS FOR LEARNING TO READ IN THE UNDER-3S

Most children who come to nursery at 3 have already developed the foundations for learning to read. According to Marion Whitehead (1996), there are two main areas of development that are the roots of literacy:

- the drive to make sense of things
- the use of symbols, representations and mark-making.

The drive to make sense of things

From birth, babies are trying to make sense of the world around them. As their physical skills develop they explore their environment. As soon as they can hold onto objects, they put them into their mouths. They taste, smell, and use their eyes, ears and sense of touch to give them information about the object they are handling. Through their contact with parents, family, friends and carers they explore the social world and they begin to be able to predict events. As children explore, they will inevitably come into contact with **environmental print** and will try to make sense of this in the same way that they try to make sense of other aspects of their environment.

In the activity above, you probably thought of:

- books, magazines and papers
- correspondence
- print on the TV and on computers
- packets and packaging
- words on clothes and labels
- words on toys and baby equipment
- words found on household appliances
- street signs, buses and advertising hoardings
- shop fronts and shop windows, supermarkets and garages.

The list is endless. A child born into our society today is surrounded by print. Children actively try to understand and make sense of what they see, in the same way that they try to make sense of everything else in their environment. Research has shown that children under 3 notice the print around them and ask questions about it.

THINK ABOUT IT

Make a list of all the situations in which a child will come into contact with print.

DEFINITION

environmental print   the printed words that are found in the world around us, other than books and newspapers, for instance street names and shop signs

---

Environmental print

THINK ABOUT IT

In the nursery situation, what activities could be provided to encourage children's use and understanding of symbols?

DEFINITIONS

representations
internalised thoughts that help us think about and recall things and people in their absence

mark-making the act of making marks which involves 'creativity, communication and some degree of permanence' (Marion Whitehead)

Symbols

As children grow older they begin to use and understand symbols. Symbols can be cultural, having the same meaning for a distinct group of people, such as the use of language. Symbols can also be personal, having a significance just for us, such as the special meaning of a song or a piece of music.

Representations

Although symbols stand in the place of something else, for instance a number for an amount, ultimately symbols stand in the place of, or represent, thoughts. Our thoughts can also be regarded as **representations**. Representations help us think about and remember events and people in their absence and help us make connections with similar events. If a young child sees a picture of a ball in a book, she might recognise it and connect it with her toy ball, which she points to. The child might also say the word *ball* or make some marks on paper and say that she has drawn a ball. The child's ability to connect a picture with an object and a word shows that she has representations about the object.

Mark-making

Children begin to make marks, often accidentally, by drawing their finger through their food, or smearing mud on a wall. Children find **mark-making** very satisfying and will repeat it for fun. Later, mark-making will become an act of communication and will progress to drawing and writing.

With these roots of literacy in mind we can begin to think of practical ways of introducing children to reading.

GOOD PRACTICE

- Good language development is the foundation for learning to read. Provide experiences to promote this.
- Read to babies from birth. Babies enjoy the rhythms of nursery rhymes and the close contact with the reader. Later, when they can hold things, babies will enjoy having books to play with. Provide cloth books, board books and bath books. From 9 months or earlier babies will begin to look at the images in books.
- Children will often want to hear the same story over and over again. This builds confidence and familiarity with words and is obviously fun and enjoyable.
- Share books with children every day. There may be set times such as bedtime, but other times of the day are equally valuable.
- Encourage older brothers and sisters, grandparents and other relatives to read to the child.

- Children who are brought up seeing their parents and carers enjoying reading are more likely to enjoy reading when they get older. In day care or nursery establishments, children should be allowed to see the staff reading for pleasure, perhaps seeing their key worker enjoying a good book during a break, or whilst the other children are sleeping.
- Young children can join a library. Many libraries have story times for under-3s and a regular trip to the library can become an event to look forward to for both adult and child.
- Singing and rhymes not only help with language development but also contribute to learning to read, because they help children see patterns in words.
- Bring to the child's attention examples of environmental print, let them 'help' you write shopping lists and ask for their help in 'reading' the list in the supermarket.

Children who have early experiences of reading have the best chance of success at school

How to read a book to a child under 3

- Show her the pictures and talk about what she is seeing, as if telling a story or reminding her of what she knows.
- Make sure that the child can reach the book, demonstrate how to turn the pages and let her take turns in page turning.
- The experience should be playful and enjoyable. Stop as soon as the child shows signs of inattention or not enjoying the process.
- Books about colours, shapes, familiar objects and events, and distinctive characters, who are recognised when the book is read again, are best.
- From time to time let the child take the initiative by encouraging her to open the book at a favourite page.
- Sometimes run your finger under the words as you read them so that the child begins to learn that, in English, print is read from left to right and from the top of the page to the bottom of the page.

✔ PROGRESS CHECK

1 What is environmental print?
2 What is a symbol?
3 Describe why a child's use of symbols is a foundation for learning to read.
4 What is a good age to introduce books to babies?
5 Describe how you would read a book to a baby of 1 year old.

DEVELOPING EARLY LITERACY IN THE 3–5S

Recognising children's skills

It is important to recognise and value the skills children may already have. By 3 or 4 years of age most children already have an understanding of what reading is and the many different circumstances in which reading takes place. The amount of understanding depends on how much they have been read to, as well as the literacy levels within the child's family, together with the experience of print the child may have acquired in day care. The child who sees parents, family members and carers enjoying reading will already be at a great advantage compared to children who have not had such an experience. According to Ann Browne (1998), most children of this age have begun to understand that:

- print carries messages that are understood by the reader
- texts carry information or stories
- texts can be responded to
- spoken language can be represented by written language
- there are different sorts of texts
- reading is a useful and important activity
- reading can be enjoyable.

In addition most children are beginning to understand how to handle books and in which direction print is read. This understanding has emerged gradually, without formal teaching and is known as **emergent literacy**.

In the nursery years the role of the adult is to build on the knowledge of reading that the child already has and to devise a curriculum for reading that not only introduces her to the skills she will need, but also helps her to widen her understanding about the various purposes of reading.

In the previous section we saw that young children have a basic drive to make sense of the world. This need to make sense of their environment applies just as much to printed material as to anything else. According to Marion Whitehead (1996), young children are more likely to investigate and learn about print if three conditions are met:

- The print must be genuine.
- The situation supports play.
- The method is scientific.

The print is genuine

Children need to be surrounded by genuine printed material. Although they benefit from material specially produced for their age group, for instance, books, and computer software designed to teach children the alphabet, phonics and spelling, their real motivation for wanting to learn to read comes in wanting to be like adults and do what adults do. Genuine print is everywhere and includes calendars, catalogues, brochures, etc. Children must be given the opportunity to investigate the real print that is found in the community around them. Most children go through a stage where their favourite reading material is a shopping catalogue which is filled with pictures, especially the toy section.

DEFINITION

emergent literacy the beginning stages of reading and writing where the child develops an awareness of printed material without formal teaching

---

THINK ABOUT IT

What examples of genuine print could you supply in a nursery situation?

THINK ABOUT IT

How can adults support children's play when they are investigating print, in a nursery situation?

The situation supports play

It is well accepted that children learn through play. However, there is confusion about what is meant by 'play'. Often the word is used to mean that a learning situation is fun. 'Play' is a term used to describe a particular form of children's activity. Play is not usually adult directed, rather it is something carried out for its own sake and the activities are their own reward. Children often play at being readers and writers when they are investigating print. The role of the adult is to value this and provide an environment and resources to make this possible, for instance providing note pads and recipe books in the home area. It is also important that the adult values what the children do, and does not make them feel foolish for getting things wrong.

DEFINITION

hypothesis   a theory about something that is not yet proved but which serves as a basis for further research

The method is scientific

When investigating new situations, young children behave like scientists. That is, they will make up an **hypothesis** (a theory) of what something means and will try to confirm that their idea is correct. For example, a child may have seen the 'open' sign on a shop door and then sees the word at a petrol station. The child has an idea or hypothesis that the word says 'open' and will seek to confirm this, probably by asking the adult she is with. Adults need to pay attention to what young children are saying and answer their questions.

Scientists also observe what happens in different situations. When children are investigating print, they need to observe adults reading in various situations. For example, children need to see adults reading instructions, reading out the register, making and reading shopping lists, reading and writing greetings cards, filling in forms, and so forth. Children need the opportunity to join in, for instance by adding their own marks and reading out lists.

Children need the opportunity to join in, for example with writing shoppling lists

Early predictors of success in learning to read

As in learning to talk or learning to walk, there are great individual differences in the speed at which children acquire the skills needed to learn to read. Research has identified some factors that influence children's reading development. One of the main factors is the child's ability to tell the difference between the different sounds found in words, as well as an ability to put these sounds together in different combinations. Because of this, learning to read cannot be seen in isolation from language development. There is a strong connection between children who have a language delay or a language disorder, and difficulties in learning to read. In addition a child needs to be able to hear well, and any significant degree of hearing impairment will affect the child's ability to learn to read.

The Sheffield Early Literacy Association looked at a group of children who were identified as being 'natural readers'. The following factors were identified as contributing to their success:

- early exposure to language and print
- sharing books with adults where they joined in actively, rather than just listening
- having favourite stories read to them over and over again
- pretend reading
- memorising a story
- having stories read aloud – not just until the child becomes a competent reader, but beyond
- reading activities where the child is encouraged to take the initiative, with the adult taking a supportive role
- developing personal libraries.

The skills children need in order to be able to read

Ann Browne (1998) identifies six basic skills that children need when learning to read:

- *phonic knowledge* – the understanding of the relationship between the sounds in the English language and print symbols
- *graphic knowledge* – the understanding that the shape of letters and patterns of letters provides information that enables the reader to extract meaning from the text. Graphic knowledge emphasises the visual aspect of print and includes an understanding of punctuation
- *word recognition skills* – the ability to recognise some words automatically, once learned. Probably the first word to be learned in this way will be the child's name
- *grammatical skills* – understanding the rules that govern the way that words are put together. Chapter 3 shows how young children begin to develop an understanding of grammar. Children bring their knowledge of grammar with them when they begin to read and this helps them extract the meaning from text

- *bibliographic skills* – knowing how texts are organised, for instance that in English text is read from left to right and from top to bottom. Knowing that an English book starts at the front. Knowing that valuable information can be gained from illustrations. Knowing the different layouts of poetry books compared with fact books, and so forth. Older children develop an understanding of contents lists, etc.

- *contextual skills* – the ability of children to apply what they already know about the world, and their previous experience as speakers and listeners, to make informed predictions about the meaning of a text.

Practical ways of encouraging the development of reading in the nursery

The book area

This should be a comfortable, carpeted area, in a quiet part of the nursery. Consideration should be made to lighting and partitioning. The area needs to be visible to adults, for safety reasons, but should give a feeling of enclosure. There needs to be comfortable seating for children and adults, for instance sofas and beanbags, and enough space for a group of children to sit together whilst an adult reads a story. Storage of books needs to be well thought out. Books need to be displayed so that children can reach them easily and the display needs to be attractive so that children will want to take them off the shelves. The books also need to be kept in good condition. Children will not be attracted to damaged, ragged books that are left in a jumble in a box. The staff team, together with the children, need to agree on a set of 'rules' to help keep the books in good condition. Some books should be changed regularly, to complement familiar old favourites. In the book area you can consider setting up a display area where books related to the current topic in the nursery are attractively arranged. Links to home can be encouraged by letting children take a book home to share with their parents/carers.

The listening area

This is best set up near the book area. The area should contain a robust tape recorder with head phones so that children can listen to tapes. The tapes may be commercially produced to go with specific books, which of course should be stored together with the tape, or tapes that the children make themselves of stories. Some nurseries place story props and boards in this area for the children to use.

Choosing books

There needs to be a variety of different types of books:

- picture books with different amounts of print, some just pictures or high-quality photographs, others with more text, designed to be read by an adult to children

- large format books designed to be used with a group of children

- books designed to encourage interaction, for instance, flap books, pop-up books and books with questions to answer

- story books and fact books

- poetry books and books of rhymes

- books from around the world showing different places and in different languages
- books that reflect cultural diversity
- dual language books that develop an awareness that English is not the only language in which books can be written – children whose first language is not English benefit if dual language books are included, written in the language they speak at home as well as English
- books that reflect diverse family types
- books designed to support children who are experiencing a variety of life events
- books where children with special needs are seen in active roles
- books that the children have written themselves
- photo albums with pictures of recent events in the nursery.

The list is endless, but the principle is that children should be exposed to a wide variety of different kinds of books that cater for their interests and allow for a wide range of reading ability.

In addition, there are certain criteria that you need to bear in mind when choosing books:

- The book must be attractive so the child wants to take it off the shelf and look at it.
- The content must be well written and interesting or entertaining to the child.
- The language must be understandable for the child, or written in such a way that the rhythms are attractive. For instance children love nonsense rhymes.
- The illustrations must be of good quality and help the child understand the text.
- If the book is non-fiction, it must be factually accurate and up-to-date.
- The books must not only be free from bias and stereotyping, but should endeavour to show people who are at risk of discrimination in positive and active roles. For instance, you would expect to see illustrations that showed children or adults with disabilities in active roles, not just as bystanders or being looked after.
- Some nurseries have books that have been written and published in other countries. They are particularly useful if they are written in languages other than English or depict scenes of everyday life or well known stories from different countries.
- Books of poor quality should not be included.

Sharing books with children

In the nursery there should be opportunities for an adult to share books with one or two children. Sometimes a child may just want the adult to read the story straight through so that she can be a passive recipient. There is nothing wrong with this, especially if you think the child needs some 'time out' to rest

DO THIS!

If you are working in a nursery, carry out this activity with the nursery team. If you are in a classroom situation, carry out this activity with other students.

1 In a group, draw up a list of criteria that you would look for in a book that is to go in a book area in a nursery.

2 Turn these criteria into a checklist.

3 Choose five books at random from the books you find in the book area where you work, or where you are on placement, and use the checklist to see if you would have chosen these books if you were buying them today.

4 Write a report outlining your conclusions and discuss your findings with the nursery team and/or other students at college.

and relax. At other times you can encourage active participation by the child by asking her to identify objects and characters, to predict what happens next, encouraging her to identify with the character by asking the child how she thinks the character feels. Occasionally as you read, you can run your finger along the text so the child develops the understanding that, in English, the text is written from left to right and goes from the top to the bottom of the page. You can also encourage the child to point out words that are repeated over and over again in the text by asking them 'which word do you think says…?'

- Encourage children to choose the books to be read. Ask them why they have chosen that particular book.

- Children often enjoy 'reading' books to each other. Sometimes a child will be the 'teacher' and retell the story to the other child, or the children will explore the text and illustrations together.

- You can help children learn about the different types of books in the book area by helping them explore what's available. With one or two children, look through the display, comment on what you find by saying things like 'Look, here's a book full of nursery rhymes', 'Look this one is all about animals'. Encourage the children to search for specific books by saying thing like 'Can you find a book about cars?' As you do this try to increase the children's vocabulary by talking, for instance, about the book's cover and the 'first page'.

- Use books to help prepare children for events that are going to happen, such as a planned trip to hospital or the imminent birth of a brother or sister. Books can also be used to help a child understand events that have happened, not only sad events like the death of a pet, but also happy events such as a trip to the seaside.

Stories

Stories can be oral or written and are accounts of imaginary or past events. Humans have used stories from the beginning of recorded time. They have been used to pass on knowledge and history from one generation to another, with much of a society's culture and religion being passed down via stories.

Stories have an important role for children, both to entertain and to educate. Stories have a familiar structure with which children become familiar at an early age. They learn that stories have a beginning, a middle and an end. Children become familiar with the difference between 'Once upon a time…', 'When Grandma was four years old…' and 'Yesterday when I went shopping…'. Each sets a different scene and communicates to the listener the type of tale they might be going to hear. Children usually come to school having an understanding of the complex nature of storytelling and it is this knowledge that helps them extract meaning from the texts to which they are exposed. This knowledge helps them when they start to write their own stories.

The value of using stories with children

- Stories give children information in ways that are easily accessible, provided that the material is appropriate to the children's stage of development.

- Stories provide a way of increasing vocabulary, and a knowledge of how sentences are constructed.
- Stories can be used to teach across the curriculum, for instance the City of Sheffield Education Department have identified a number of children's books that can be used to introduce scientific concepts.
- Stories can be used to help children come to terms with major life events, for instance the birth of a brother or sister, or a planned trip to hospital.
- Children can learn about their culture and religion through stories, and can be introduced to the culture and religion of others.
- Stories are a source of great enjoyment.

Story time

Many nurseries have times set aside in the routine of the day for story time with small or large groups of children. There are varying opinions about the value of taking a large group of children for story time. For younger children it is probably more appropriate to have small groups for story time.

Story time is very valuable and can consist of a child-care practitioner either telling a story or reading a story from a book. Both activities are skills that need to be practised. Child-care students will need to observe experienced staff to see what strategies they use to keep the children's attention and transmit the story. At first students will need to practise on their own at home and then carry out story time with small groups of children, before building up to larger groups. However shy you feel, it is a good idea to have an experienced member of staff observing you to help with your technique.

Story time is very valuable

Reading a book in story time

- When reading a story choose a book that you enjoy and read through it so that you are familiar with the contents. When reading it through to yourself, you can assess its suitability for the group you will be reading it to. Has it got the right balance of text to illustration for the age group? Is the language accessible to the children? Whilst reading through the book, practise any sound effects you will make and any words or sentences you will emphasise or repeat.

- If the story time is not in the book area, it needs to be in an area that is quiet (not in a main thoroughfare), well lit and free from draughts. The children need to be able to sit on a clean, carpeted area around you. There needs to be enough space so they are comfortable, but small enough to give the children a feeling of containment. The adult needs to sit on a comfortable chair, positioned in such a way that the children can see. Everything needed for the session should be at hand and it should be arranged that there will be no interruptions. In order to achieve this there needs to be a team approach to planning the nursery day, with the facility to be flexible when necessary.

- Before you start make sure all the children are settled and you have their attention. Explore the cover of the book with the children, ask them if they have any idea what the book may be about and tell them why you have chosen it (a favourite, or linked to events in the nursery, etc.).

- When you read the story give the children plenty of time to absorb what they are hearing and to look at the illustrations. You will have to know the story very well so that you turn the book round for all the children to see the illustrations. As you read, emphasise the drama of the story by using pauses and silences. Encourage the children to join in with repetitions and sound effects. Don't be afraid to ask the children what they think might happen next or how a character might be feeling. Whilst reading the story occasionally run your fingers along the text reinforcing directionality and point out words that occur often within the text.

- When you have finished the book, give the children an opportunity to tell you what they thought about it. Go through the book again, pointing to the illustrations and encouraging the children to retell the story. You may be able to link the story to suitable nursery rhymes which will reinforce the children's vocabulary. The book can then be placed in an accessible position so that the children can look at it again when they want to. Some books have tapes that accompany them and these should be available.

Telling a story

You don't always have to read from a book at story time. Well known stories like 'Goldilocks and the Three Bears' can be told from memory. Traditional stories often have strong, repetitive language which will encourage the children to join in. Children enjoy hearing stories about what happened to the adult when they were young, or stories where the children themselves are included as characters. Telling stories helps children develop their imagination because they haven't got any pictures to look at.

Story props

Story props are a valuable tool in keeping children's attention during the telling of a story or whilst a book is being read. They are also useful for children to use on their own or with each other to help them retell the story and is an aid to developing sequencing skills.

Story props are made by copying or cutting out pictures of characters and key events in a story. These pictures can be put on card and laminated. If you have access to a magnetic board, a magnetic strip can be placed on the back of the story prop, or the story prop can be attached to a board with Blu-tack.® As the story is being read the adult places the props on the board. An alternative method is to make puppets of the main characters that the children can use to help retell the story. Story props can also include objects that are easily available and which reinforce an aspect of the story being told. For instance bowls and spoons for the Three Bears or a bucket and spade for a story about the seaside.

Storysacks

These arose from an idea of Neil Griffiths, an former headteacher, and are related to story props. A typical storysack consists of a drawstring bag that contains:

- an illustrated story book suitable for the children's age
- one or more toys representing main characters from the book
- relevant story props, for instance spoons in different sizes for the story of 'Goldilocks and the Three Bears'
- a non-fiction book that is connected to the story book. For instance, 'Goldilocks and the Three Bears' could be accompanied by a book about bears or a book that helps children understand the concepts of 'big, bigger, biggest'
- an audio tape of the story book
- a set of 'instructions', giving parents and other adults suggestions as to how to use the storysack.

Contents of storysacks can vary. Other suggestions include:

- a language game connected to the main theme of the storysack
- a mini stage set or playmat depicting the different settings in which the story takes place. For instance, in the Three Bears story, a play mat might show Goldilocks' home, the forest, the Bears' cottage, the Bears' kitchen and the Bears' bedroom
- a maths game, for instance a game encouraging children to match each bowl to each bear
- simple board games using dice and counters that are designed around the theme of the book
- matching cards
- puppets.

DO THIS!

Make a storysack. Try using it with a child or a group of children.

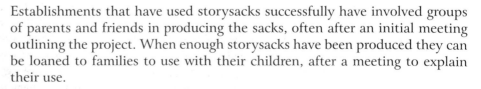

Establishments that have used storysacks successfully have involved groups of parents and friends in producing the sacks, often after an initial meeting outlining the project. When enough storysacks have been produced they can be loaned to families to use with their children, after a meeting to explain their use.

Sequencing

After you have read through a book for the first time with the children, you can go over the text again. This time draw key scenes from the text onto card.

Later the children can try to put the cards in the correct order to retell the story. Alternatively, you could photocopy pages from the book and laminate them so that the children can use them in the same way. When you go on nursery trips, or when there is an important event within the nursery, take a series of photographs. These can be mounted on card and laminated. The children are then encouraged to put the photographs in order to retell the event. Sequencing activities can be undertaken with individual children, in small groups or with pairs of children retelling the event to each other.

The use of poetry and rhymes

As well as stories, children should be introduced to poetry and rhymes. There are poems and rhymes that have been specifically written to appeal to young children, but poetry that one would associate with older children or adults can also be enjoyed by children if it has rhythm and is read or recited with a sense of drama. In the same way, children also enjoy poetry and rhymes in other languages.

It is always more successful if adults introduce children to poetry that they like themselves, since the adult's enjoyment will communicate itself to the children.

Children should be given the opportunity to compose their own poetry, even at nursery age, and will often experiment spontaneously with nonsense words or novel combinations of words and rhythm. Adults should encourage and respect these early experiments with language.

Imaginative play areas

The imaginative play area can be used to support reading. The home area can contain examples of reading material often found in the children's homes, such as telephone directories, calendars, note pads, appointment cards, catalogues from stores and holiday firms, diaries, maps, bills, etc. There should be writing material for children to write notes and letters.

Areas can be set up to reflect current themes in the nursery. An area set up as a doctor's surgery, an office or a hair salon all give opportunities for the children to experience printed materials in a realistic way. Imaginative play areas can be set up to resemble a scene from a favourite book. Appropriate props can encourage the children to act out the story. These areas need to be changed frequently to retain their attraction and are ideal opportunities to involve staff, parents and children in a joint activity.

Apart from its value in supporting literacy, role-play can contribute to children's development in a variety of ways. It can:

- reinforce previous learning about events and situations in children's lives
- help children come to terms with major life events
- help children gain information, for instance the provision of clothes from other cultures for the children to wear will help children know more about that culture
- allow children to communicate thoughts and feelings in a way that would not be possible through the use of language at that stage of development

GOOD PRACTICE

- Adults should encourage children to play with words.
- Give suggestions for words children could use, words that might rhyme or repetitions.
- Stimulate the children by reading and reciting a wide variety of poetry and rhymes.
- Write down the children's efforts at writing poetry.
- Suggest that children illustrate their poems.
- Record children's poetry and listen to it together.
- Older children can be introduced to the concept of drafting and redrafting their work.

- help children to learn the skill of interacting with others
- help them become aware of the needs of others.

Displays

Displays of children's work, interest tables, book displays and so forth, all present opportunities for displaying text around the nursery. It is essential that great care is taken over the lettering. Always mount text and use suitable colours that make the text stand out. Use lower case letters, except when upper case is appropriate. The lettering must be big enough to be seen from a distance and it goes without saying that the text must be correctly spelt. You can use a computer to create and print out text for displays.

Labels and signs

Take every opportunity to clearly label aspects of the nursery environment. Label cupboards, drawers and containers to tell the children what is in them. Clearly label the different areas of the nursery, such as the exits and the home area.

Children's pegs, drawers and lockers

Ask the children to bring in photographs of themselves and use these together with labels with their name, clearly printed, to identify their coat peg, drawers and lockers.

Activities and games to encourage reading skills

- Whenever you prepare for an activity, let the children see you write out a list of what you need. Let them help you gather the materials. The children can help you read the list to see if you have everything, ticking off the items as they are assembled.
- Help the children make books. This could be a book for an individual child where, for instance, they draw a picture of each member of their family. Each picture is clearly named and put together in book form with a title page. Whole-class books can be made with each child drawing a picture about an event which is labelled appropriately. These books need to be robust and can be kept on display in the book area.
- Children can be encouraged to recognise their name by having a supply of laminated name labels that they can use to put by their place at dinner or under a completed piece of craft work or to be used in games where children are encouraged to match various name labels to photographs of children in their class.
- Phonic awareness can be encouraged by introducing children to a wide variety of rhymes, rhythms and patterns in speech. Use riddles, tongue twisters, nursery rhymes, songs and poems.
- Play games such as 'I spy'.
- Encourage children to clap out the rhythms in their names to help them become aware of syllables.
- Read a variety of alphabet books with the children.

There are, of course, many more activities that can be planned to help children develop reading skills.

Planning

It is not possible to deliver an effective curriculum without planning. When thinking about one aspect of the curriculum, such as reading, it is important to realise that this is unlikely to be delivered as an isolated subject. In the nursery age group the reading curriculum can be integrated within other areas. For instance, a cooking activity that is primarily designed to help the child with scientific concepts will also give the opportunity for number work as well as reading the list of ingredients and the recipe. Practically every activity in the nursery can be modified to help develop reading skills.

Assessment

It is important that a child's developing skills are assessed at regular intervals. It is only when you have a good idea of what a child can do, that you can plan appropriate goals and learning activities. Regular assessment will give you feedback as to whether the child is progressing well, or if you need to modify your plans because there is a difficulty in some area.

There are two basic ways to assess children's developing reading skills. One is direct observation. As you share and discuss a book with a child (or by observing another adult with the child), you can get a lot of information about the child's skills. You may be able to note that the child is able to retell the story using the pictures, that she has an awareness of the directionality of print, that she is able to point out words that are repeated and recognise some words. She may be able to point out the first letter of her name when it occurs in the text. After the book is finished, you need to jot these observations down in a notebook to be written up more fully later.

Another method is the checklist method where you have a tick list of skills and observe that child over a period of a day or two during her normal nursery activities to see if she displays these skills. The checklist method is useful because it is easy to use and can be carried out at various times during the year to check the child's progress. You can devise your own checklist or purchase a ready-made scheme which is especially designed for nurseries. The skills in your checklist could, for instance, include holding a book appropriately, turning pages correctly, knowing the directionality of print, retelling a story from memory, being able to put pictures in a sequence to tell a story, recognising some letters, recognising her name, and being able to read labels.

The whole nursery team should be involved in discussions about the methods of assessment to use and that assessment is linked into the cycle of planning. In addition, it is important not to forget that the children's parents are a valuable source of information about the children's developing reading skills.

CASE STUDY

Jason

Jason is 3½. He has just entered a community nursery, attending five days a week from 8.30 a.m. until 5.30 p.m. He is an only child and lives with his mother, teenage aunt and uncle and his grandmother. The family is loving and supportive and Jason is the centre of their attention. Jason's key worker carries out a pre-visit to the family's home. One of the things the family discuss with the key worker is their concern about helping Jason learn to read. Jason's mother tells the key worker that she has always had problems with reading, but that the other family members are able to read.

1 What advice could the key worker give Jason's family about helping develop his reading skills at home?

2 How could Jason's key worker support the family in the coming year?

3 How can the key worker support Jason's reading in nursery?

✔ PROGRESS CHECK

1 What knowledge about reading may a child of 3 already possess?

2 What skills do children need to become efficient readers?

3 In what conditions are young children more likely to investigate print?

4 What criteria would you use when choosing books for a book area?

5 Why is it important to use rhymes and poems with children?

DEVELOPING READING SKILLS IN THE 5–7S (SCHOOL AGE)

On entry to statutory schooling, the responsibility for teaching children to read traditionally lies with the class teacher. In many schools there is a team approach with child-care practitioners, such as nursery nurses and classroom assistants, working in the classroom alongside the teacher. Parents often play an active role, not only helping their children at home, but also acting as volunteers within the classroom. In this section, we look at ways adults can support children's reading development when they start school.

Baseline assessment

When children enter school, within the first term, an assessment is made of their reading ability. This assessment is used as a basis for planning suitable learning activities for each child and as a benchmark to help monitor children's progress throughout the school system.

Although there is great variation in ability, it is expected that, by the time most children enter school at five, they should be able to hold a book appropriately, turn the pages and retell a story from memory, recognise their own name and recite familiar rhymes. A very few children will be able to read simple texts, recognise all the letters by shape and sound and demonstrate a knowledge of sound sequences in words.

The National Curriculum

In England, once children are in statutory schooling (i.e. from Year 1), they follow the National Curriculum. This is not intended to be a static scheme and there are changes every few years. It is important that child-care practitioners working with school-aged children have an up-to-date knowledge of requirements.

By the time children are at the end of Year 2, when most are 7, those of 'average ability' will probably be able to read simple texts accurately, with understanding. They will be able to use a variety of ways to help them understand text:

- phonics (recognising the sounds of letters and letter combinations)
- graphics (knowing the shape of letters and words)
- syntax (knowing the way words are used [word order] to form meaningful phrases and sentences)
- context (using pictures and other clues such as knowledge of the subject).

Children should also be able to express opinions about what they have read in stories, poems and non-fiction.

Recommended methods for teaching reading in schools

Earlier in the chapter we looked at various models of reading and at various methods derived from these models. At the moment, the recommended method is an interactionist approach where children are introduced to reading at the word, sentence and text level. The six skills, of phonics, graphical skills, word recognition skills, grammatical skills, bibliographic skills and contextual skills, that children need to acquire in order to learn to read, and which are discussed earlier, are also reflected in current recommendations.

It is recommended that children are taught phonics from the beginning (i.e. in Reception classes) and it is recommended that children are taught to:

- discriminate between the separate sounds in words
- learn the letters and letter combinations most commonly used to spell those sounds
- read words by sounding out and blending their separate parts
- write words by combining the spelling patterns of their sounds.

The Literacy Hour

Since September 1998 all classes in England from Reception to Year 6 have been required to dedicate an hour a day for the teaching of literacy. The Literacy Hour has been set in place so that there is:

- continuity of practices within schools
- effective use of time
- an emphasis on class and group work rather than individualised teaching
- high-quality literacy instruction
- effective class management.

The management of the literacy hour follows government guidelines, with elements of whole-class teaching, small group work and children working on their own. Children work at both their reading and writing skills in this hour. If you are involved in the Literacy Hour, you should make sure that you keep up-to-date with current requirements.

Partnership with parents

An important part of helping children develop their reading skills in school is an effective partnership with the children's parents. As well as using parents as volunteers within the classroom, schools are recommended to set up home–school contracts, regular reading homework, workshops and meetings with parents to discuss reading.

How parents and other adults can support children's reading

Parents, relatives and friends can help children by reinforcing what they are learning at school. The following points may be helpful. They have been taken from Department for Education and Employment (DfEE) advice to parents as part of the National Year of Reading scheme.

- All children are different. When listening to a child read, respond to her needs and let her read at her own pace.
- Some children need to be encouraged to slow down with their reading and look carefully at each word. Others need to move the story along and not to worry so much about their mistakes.
- If a child gets stuck encourage her to use all the information available to her to make a guess. Encourage her to look at the pictures and remember what has happened in the story.
- Read a story together, then read it again, missing out words. Get the child to fill in the blanks. A different word that means the same thing may be suggested. That's good as it shows that the child is thinking about the story and the words.
- Help the child see that she already knows the biggest part of words like *play-ing*, *eat-en*, by breaking the word down. If she reads out the part she knows you can finish it for her.
- Help with long words by clapping along together or counting out the different chunks of the word (for example, three for *tram-po-line*).
- When the child reads and gets a word wrong, let her finish the line before you put her right. Children often realise what the word should be and go back and correct themselves.
- It's important to offer support if the child needs to practise things over and over again.

- Make the most of the books that the child brings home from school. Read them yourself and talk about them to the child.
- Check that the child is following what she is reading by asking her to tell you the story in her own words.
- Allow the child to re-read familiar stories, or to hear you re-read them. Knowing a familiar book will help her notice more about the words on the page and she will start to recognise the patterns in new words and stories.
- Listen to stories learned by heart and encourage the child to re-tell them in her own words or even act them out.
- Buy books as presents instead of toys.
- Find books about something you know they like.
- Set up a special place for books from the library or their own books.

By reading with children, parents, relatives and friends can help to reinforce what they are learning at school

CASE STUDY

Indrani and Clare

Indrani and Clare are the teacher and nursery nurse in a Reception class of a primary school in a multi-ethnic, inner-city area. They have noticed that many of the parents are reluctant to get involved with teaching their children to read. They suspect that some parents are worried about their own lack of reading skills, some parents are not yet fluent in English and some parents have expressed the opinion that teaching children to read is the teacher's job, not theirs. Indrani and Clare want to strengthen their partnership with the children's parents.

1 Make a list of other possible reasons for parents' reluctance to become involved.

2 What strategies could Indrani and Clare use to involve more parents?

Boys and reading

In general, boys have poorer reading skills than girls. The differences can be seen as early as nursery class and continue to school-leaving age where only a third of boys achieve a higher grade GCSE in English compared with half the girls. It is thought that boys often see books as boring or unmasculine and that their reading preferences are sometimes ignored.

Experienced child-care practitioners often observe that whereas girls prefer story books and novels when they are older, boys seem to prefer factual books, joke books and books that scare them. It is vital that boys are offered books that appeal to them in the important years when they are learning to read.

GOOD PRACTICE

- Ensure boys see men enjoying reading: invite fathers into school to hear children read; encourage male friends and relatives to read to children at home.
- Point out to children books that are written by male authors. If possible, arrange for children to meet a male author in person.
- Do not be negative about what boys choose to read. Any reading is acceptable at this stage, whether it is the football results or toy catalogues. Encourage boys to read magazines and comics.
- Boys often enjoy fiction that features adventure and sport and this should be a consideration when selecting books for children.
- Books of jokes, funny poems, riddles and nonsense poems are often enjoyed by boys and should be made available to them.
- Children are often motivated to read by going to the cinema or watching TV. Try to have books that relate to current favourites for the children to read.
- Most boys like to read books that scare them. Many publishers produce series of 'spine chillers'. If children enjoy one book in a series, they may be encouraged to read the rest.
- Try to find out what hobbies the children have and find books about these subjects.
- When choosing books to read to the class, do not just read fiction, but include some of the other kinds of books that boys enjoy.

✔ PROGRESS CHECK

1 What methods are recommend for the teaching of reading?
2 Describe the activities in the Literacy Hour.
3 If you are hearing a child read, how can you help if they get stuck on a word?

KEY TERMS

You need to know the meaning of the following words and phrases. Go back through the chapter to make sure you understand them:

emergent literacy
environmental print
hypothesis
mark-making
reading
representations

FURTHER READING

Browne, A. (1998) *A Practical Guide to Teaching Reading in the Early Years*, Paul Chapman
This is an excellent book, full of practical suggestions that are useful both for child-care practitioners and students at levels three and four.

Morris, J. and Mort, L. (1992) *Beginning to Read: Bright Ideas for Early Years*, Scholastic
A practical book which all students will find useful. The book gives many ideas for activities.

Whitehead, M. (1996) *The Development of Language and Literacy*, Hodder & Stoughton
This book is useful for students on level three and four courses.

Whitehead, M. (1999) *Supporting Language and Literacy Development in the Early Years*, Open University Press
Child-care practitioners and students on level three and four courses will find the descriptions of good practice in nurseries very useful.

Yates, I. (1998) *Language and Literacy*, Learning in the Early Years series, Scholastic
This book is useful for students on child-care and education courses.

The development of writing

The key topics covered in this chapter are:

- What is writing?
- The role of physical and perceptual development in writing
- The foundations for learning to write in the under-3s
- Developing writing skills in the 3–5s
- Developing writing skills in the 5–7s.

In this chapter we investigate how children learn to write. However, reading and writing are strongly related to each other and although it is convenient to look at the two processes separately, in reality the development of reading and writing proceed hand-in-hand.

Most children enjoy playing with pencils and coloured pens. They explore and experiment with enthusiasm. If children see a wide variety of written material in their environment and see adults writing, they will be motivated to develop these skills for themselves.

In this chapter we look at how parents and child-care practitioners can support children as they develop their writing skills.

WHAT IS WRITING?

Writing consists of taking the sounds of oral language and changing them into symbols that are able to be recorded permanently and can be read when the person who communicated the message is no longer there. Handwriting, computer print, Egyptian hieroglyphics and Braille can all be considered forms of writing.

THINK ABOUT IT

Look at the following list and identify the items that you would consider to come under the category of 'writing':

- Spoken English
- Egyptian hieroglyphics
- British Sign Language (see Chapter 8)
- Braille (see Chapter 8)
- Makaton (see Chapter 8)
- handwriting
- computer print
- morse code
- semaphore.

When you have made your list, try to identify the criteria you used to decide if an item on the list was an example of writing. If you are doing this exercise in a group situation, compare your list with others and see if you agree.

Children gradually become aware that the written symbols they see around them are related to oral language and that there are similarities between speech and writing. They learn that oral language can be converted into marks that are written down, or printed.

Comparing oral and written language

There are, of course, differences between oral language and writing:

- It is rare for writing to contain an exact version of something that was said. For instance, minutes of meetings or records of conversations are not usually word-for-word transcripts.

- A written message is not dependent on the author to be present when it is read. It can be read by many other people at different times and in different places.

- An oral communication is easily forgotten. Writing something down allows the communication to be remembered exactly and gives time for the reader to think about what has been written.

- Writing allows the author to plan exactly what they want to say. For example poets and novelists will often spend a long time organising what they want to write and will change what is written again and again until they feel that what they have written is what they want to say.

DO THIS!

1 Make a list of all the times that you write things down during a typical working day.

2 Make a list of the things that you write down during a typical day off, when you are at home.

The uses of writing

Just as children need to understand the many different situations where the ability to read is important, they also need to be introduced to the wide variety of situations where the ability to write is important.

In the activity on the left, you probably found that the list for the working day was much longer. There are very few jobs today that do not require workers to write things down at some point in the day. It is vital that the children we care for become proficient at writing because those who cannot write are at a lifelong disadvantage.

Here are just a few of the uses of writing; you will be able to think of more:

- social writing, such as sending letters, birthday cards and invitations, aimed at forging and maintaining social bonds

- home administration, such as filling in forms and writing cheques

- memory aids, such as writing down telephone messages, shopping lists, the use of calendars and diaries

- writing for a wider audience, such as writing for community newsletters and magazines, professional writing for newspapers, books and journals, and the writing of instruction manuals

- giving instructions in the form of road signs and safety notices

- using posters and print for advertising

- report writing and the writing of memos, minutes and letters in the working environment

- writing policies and procedures in the workplace

- personal writing such as using a diary, writing that is used to help us clarify our thoughts but is not meant for others to read.

In summary, there are two main functions of writing. One is to help individuals organise their thoughts, make sense of the world around them and give meaning to their experiences. The other is to communicate messages, information, thoughts and feelings to other people.

What children need to learn about writing

It should be clear from the previous section that learning to write involves more than just learning to write down the words and symbols of oral language. There is much more that needs to be learned and this process is lifelong. Many of us find that we need continually to develop our writing skills as the situations in which we find ourselves change. Among the skills that children and young people need to acquire are the ability to:

- write the individual letters of the alphabet, lower and upper case
- write using a variety of scripts, such as print and joined up writing, and the ability to use computers
- spell words correctly, and use grammar and punctuation appropriately
- write in a style that matches the function of the communication. For instance, individuals need to know how to write formal letters, business letters, social letters and letters of condolence. In preparation for employment, young people should be given the experience of taking phone messages, writing memos, taking minutes of meetings and writing reports
- write creatively in poetry and prose
- write according to academic conventions, demonstrating the ability to analyse, synthesise and order ideas in a logical way.

From the above list, we can see that the skills a child needs to acquire fall into two groups:

- **transcription** – the secretarial aspects of writing, such as spelling, punctuation and handwriting
- **composition** – the expression of ideas.

Many of us have yet to reach the highest levels of writing, but we may be caring for children who have the potential to become the great writers of the future. We must ensure that children's natural enthusiasm and excitement is continually fed so that learning to write remains a delight rather than a chore.

DEFINITIONS

transcription the secretarial aspects of writing such as spelling, punctuation and handwriting

composition the expression of ideas in writing

✔ PROGRESS CHECK

1 Explain why Braille can be considered a form of writing whilst British Sign Language cannot.

2 List four different uses for writing.

3 Children need to know how to write letters and spell words correctly. They also need to know how to write grammatically. What else do they need to know about writing?

103

THE ROLE OF PHYSICAL AND PERCEPTUAL DEVELOPMENT IN WRITING

Before a child can learn to write, certain skills and understanding must be in place. As with all aspects of education, it is essential that children's basic needs are met first. It goes without saying that when caring for children, the priority must be in ensuring that children are fit, well, safe and emotionally secure before attempting to teach them to write. This may seem self-evident, but all to often there are misguided attempts to 'teach' children to write when they are too tired, not interested or just too young to be expected to participate.

Hand–eye co-ordination

Before children can learn to write they need to develop the ability to hold a pencil appropriately and to co-ordinate vision and fine muscle movement in order to use the pencil. This is known as **hand–eye co-ordination**. At birth infants can only see clearly objects that are about 8–10 inches away from them. They have poor control over their muscles and are unable to reach out and grasp the objects that they see. Muscle control develops slowly over the first year. First the baby is able to control large muscle groups and only later the fine muscles in fingers. Researchers have observed many hundreds of babies and have found that vision and fine muscle control tend to follow a pattern. The stages of hand–eye co-ordination are summarised in Table 6.1.

Table 6.1   The stages of hand–eye co-ordination

Age	Stage of development of hand–eye co-ordination
3 months	Fists uncurl. Babies engage in finger play. Clumsy attempts made to reach objects placed in front of them.
6 months	Babies can grasp an object using their whole hand, using a **palmar grasp**. They can pass toys from one hand to another.
9 months	Babies will reach out towards small objects, index finger extended. Pick up objects using an **inferior pincer grip**.
12 months	Babies can pick up small objects using a pincer grip.
15 months	Children will hold a crayon in their whole hand using a palmer grip. Will scribble.
18 months	Children will hold a pencil halfway down its length, or at the top, using a palmar grasp or a primitive **tripod grasp**. They scribble using to and fro movements and dots. They may show that they are right or left handed. They may scribble using crayons in both hands.
2 years	Children hold pencils more towards the point, using thumb and first two fingers. They can scribble in a circular motion. Can copy a vertical line and sometimes a V shape.
2½ years	Tripod grasp has improved, **preferred hand** is used. Can copy horizontal lines, vertical lines, circles and letters T and V.
3 years	Pencil held at the point with good control, using tripod grip, using preferred hand. Can copy circles, crosses and letters V, H, T.
4 years	Pencil held in adult fashion. Can copy a cross and letters V, H, T, O.
5 years	Good control of pencils and crayons. Can copy squares and triangles (by 5½). Can copy letters V, T, H, O, X, L, A, C, U, Y. Will write some letters spontaneously.

At around 6 months, a baby grasps the object using the palmar grasp

At 1 year, a baby can pick up a pea in a pincer grasp

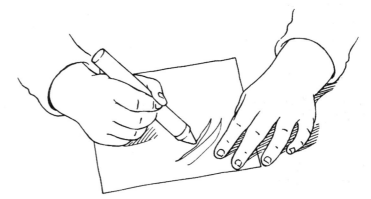

By 3 years, a child can hold a pencil in a tripod grasp

Later in the chapter we look at the development of writing in more detail. We will see that in many cases children may write letters before the ages given above, especially if the letters appear in their own name.

✔ PROGRESS CHECK

1 Why is it inappropriate to expect a baby of 9 months to copy a circle?

2 In what age range would you expect a child to be able to copy a circle?

3 In what age range would you expect a child to be able to pick up a small object using a neat pincer grasp?

4 If you give a child of 15 months a pencil, where along the length of the pencil would you expect the child to hold it?

5 A child of 5 holds a pencil in a palmar grasp. Is this usual? Explain your answer.

THINK ABOUT IT

Consider an 18-month-old child who is cared for at home by her mother. List the situations throughout a day when the child may observe someone writing.

THE FOUNDATIONS OF LEARNING TO WRITE IN THE UNDER-3S

Children gradually become aware of the relationship between written and printed words, and oral language. In addition to seeing printed material all around them at home, in the nursery and in the street, children also see adults and older children engaged in writing activities.

For the activity above, you were probably able to think of the child observing an adult writing a shopping list, jotting down a telephone message, writing a letter, writing an appointment on calendar or writing a cheque.

Through seeing adults and family members engaged in writing young children learn that this is an important activity and will begin to imitate the behaviour that they see. Ann Browne (1993) considers that young children learn three things by observing and talking to others about writing, that:

- writing is important and has a variety of different uses
- writing makes sense – they learn that in English we write from left to right and that there are recurring patterns in writing
- they, too, can communicate in writing.

Stages in learning to write

DEFINITION

developmental writing   the idea that children actively explore and experiment with writing

Children actively explore and experiment with writing, in the same way that they explore other aspects of their environment. In 1983 A.H. Dyson described this process of exploration as **developmental writing** and identified three stages through which children progress when learning to write. The role of adults is to take account of what children know and can do and to support their explorations by providing resources and relevant activities and organising the environment so that their achievements can be extended.

Stage 1
Children explore mark-making. They experiment and get satisfaction from their discoveries. They may produce lines and symbols that look like writing. Their writing at this stage does not carry a meaning.

Stage 2
Children show that they understand that writing carries a meaning. They may write letters and words but are not able to read them back. Although their own writing may not carry a message, the children show that they are aware that writing can carry a message because they ask others to read their writing to them.

Stage 3
Children decide the message they want to communicate, remember the letters they need and then write the message. At first messages are usually names of familiar people and places. Later they are change their writing to fit in with a variety of purposes and audiences.

Early mark-making

In learning to walk, children usually go through set stages. However learning to write is not quite as orderly as this. Although we have identified the general stages that are outlined above, Marie Clay (1987) considers that development of writing has more to do with the opportunity to explore print rather than intelligence or age. She has noted that children of very different ages can be seen doing similar things in their experiments with writing.

Exploring (scribble)

A child as young as 1 will make repetitive marks on paper if he is given a pen or pencil. He will also, given the opportunity, make marks in food, mud and other such media. A toddler of 15 months, given a pencil and a blank sheet of paper, will begin exploring with obvious satisfaction. The result will be what adults describe as 'scribble'. The child will make the marks and then examine them to see what he has produced. At first this 'scribble' may appear to have little in the way of a pattern, but later he will scribble in circular patterns that may be attempts at drawing, and up and down lines that may represent early attempts at writing.

Sarah has experimented with lines going round and round and from side to side

As children experiment with mark-making, they will produce some patterns that they have seen before. They begin to associate a particular hand and wrist movement with a particular pattern. They learn the movements needed to produce circular motions, lines and crosses. They also learn how to hold the paper so it doesn't slip and how much pressure is needed to make a mark with a particular pen or pencil. Towards the end of the 'scribble' stage it may be possible to notice that children with names that begin with letters made of straight lines such as *H* or *T* will use straight lines in their writing whilst children with names beginning with *S* or *C* will use circular patterns.

- Provide children with lots of opportunities to see adults writing. Explain what you are doing when you are writing. When the opportunity arises, let the children see you fill in forms, make lists and write letters.
- Take the children to places where they will see writing going on around them. Draw attention to the writing taking place at the doctor's surgery, the hairdresser, the bank and the post office.
- Provide children with opportunities for 'real' writing themselves. Let them 'sign' birthday cards, send letters to friends and family, send out their own invitations and thank you letters.
- Remember that the emphasis should be on giving opportunities for children to become writers. Deliberate attempts to teach writing to the under-3s may put too much pressure on them and they will begin to avoid writing activities. Remember that the concentration span of a child of this age may be short, so resources should be made available to them for them to use when they want to.
- Keep relaxed, try to capture some of the excitement and satisfaction that the children are getting from their experiments.
- Provide lots of resources for the children to experiment with. In a nursery there needs to be an area set aside for mark-making with tables and chairs at the correct height. But young children may also like to experiment with writing on the floor. At home, consideration needs to be given to providing space for the child and a suitable surface for writing on. Don't expect a child to use a desk in his bedroom; he is more likely to experiment in the family room with others around him.
- Provide a wide selection of non-toxic pens, pencils, coloured pencils, felt-tips and wax crayons of different colours and thickness. Children under 3 will need constant supervision when playing with pencils. Do not allow them to walk around with pencils in their mouths as some nasty injuries can be caused if they fall. Remove the tops of pens so that there is no risk of choking. Do not allow children to use pencils as weapons.
- Children do not need lined paper to write on at this age. The best paper should have plenty of blank space to write on, but that doesn't mean that you have to spend a great deal of money on new material. You can use the backs of paper that has been printed on one side, old wrapping paper, the end of wallpaper rolls (not the ready-pasted sort as this may contain toxic chemicals). Old greetings cards can also be used. Children like to experiment with paper of different colours and shapes so provide as much variety as possible.
- After a visit to the bank or the post office, you could supply examples of blank forms for the children to fill in.
- Take time to consider storage of materials. Children will not be tempted if everything is a jumble. All the resources should be accessible so that children can select what they need for themselves. You may consider using labels to identify where things are stored. This will help children develop their reading skills. Pencils and crayons need to be kept sharp. Paper needs to be stored flat. Older children may enjoy helping you keep everything tidy.
- Keep examples of the children's attempts at writing. Store them flat, in a folder or ring binder. Always put their name and the date on the sample, together with a note about the circumstances in which the writing was produced and what the child said about the writing. If the children are in a nursery, this record will be very useful for discussing the child's progress with parents and carers. A record kept by parents at home can be used in discussion with teachers in the future and will be a delightful resource for children and parents to look back on in the future.
- Provide lots of opportunities for children to develop their gross and fine motor skills. Although writing involves small muscle control, it is unlikely that children, who have yet to gain efficient use of their large muscles, will be able to co-ordinate their small muscles. Plenty of physical exercise both inside and outside is needed. Small muscle control can be encouraged by the provision of activities such as threading, fastening buttons, construction activities and small world play.

✔ PROGRESS CHECK

1 What three things do children find out about writing by observing examples of writing in their environment and by talking to adults about writing?
2 What is developmental writing?
3 What are children learning about writing when they scribble?
4 Describe three things you can do to help a child under 3 discover about writing.

DEVELOPING WRITING SKILLS IN THE 3–5S

By the time most children are 3 they already know quite a lot about writing, particularly if they have been exposed to the activities and experiences outlined in the previous section. At this age many children are attending some kind of pre-school facility for part of the day, or are in day-care.

The early years' curriculum

Establishments that provide care and education for pre-school aged children, in England, deliver a planned curriculum, based on government guidelines. These guidelines change from time to time and it is important that child-care practitioners are familiar with current advice.

By the time children leave nursery to enter statutory schooling, it expected that their writing skills will have developed sufficiently for them to be able to:

- communicate meaning through the use of pictures, symbols and some familiar words and letters
- show that they understand some of the different purposes of writing
- write their name.

Emergent writing

In the previous section we looked at the developmental model of children's writing and it was noted that in the first stage, the 'writing' does not carry a message. Gradually over the next couple of years, given appropriate opportunities and experiences, children's writing becomes more conventional. This more conventional writing is called **emergent writing**. It is not always easy to identify the onset of emergent writing as it is very gradual. It is characterised by being able to be 'read' by someone else and by the children themselves. It corresponds to stage 3 in A.H. Dyson's model of developmental writing (page 106).

The difference between drawing and writing

In the section on 'scribble' we noted that very young children appear to differentiate between drawing and writing. From lines and shapes that children have learned to produce in the 'scribble' stage emerge marks and patterns that represent things the children have seen around them. By the time children are 3 they will be able to produce something that is recognisably a drawing, and something that looks like writing. On page 110 are two pieces of work produced by Beth aged 3 years and 1 month. The first is a drawing which she described as 'Beth's face with eyes'. The second piece of work is a spontaneous piece of writing which clearly shows that she knows the difference between drawing and writing.

Changing from scribble to writing

Over time children's scribble becomes more recognisable as attempts at writing.

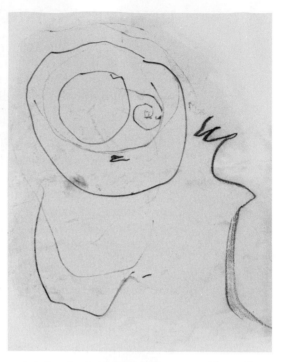

'Beth's face with eyes'. A drawing by Beth aged 3 years and 1 month

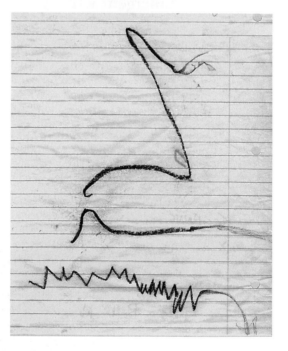

Beth's name. A piece of writing by Beth aged 3 years 1 month

Streamers

When Beth writes her name she is showing that she knows that writing goes in lines. She has produced a scribble streamer, which is one unbroken line. Often you will see children write line after line, as if they are writing a letter.

Breaking streamers into 'words'

After a period of writing unbroken streamers, children will break the line down into separate marks that show that they understand that writing is broken down into words.

This child has broken down scribble streamers into words. Some letter shapes are identifiable

Repeating patterns

The piece of writing above shows another feature of this stage of writing. The child has been repeating the same form over and over again. In this case it is an *m* shape. Children will repeat patterns in various positions and orientations.

Using letters

Gradually some of the patterns are identifiable as letters, and it is around this time that children begin to be able to recognise and name letters. The first letter they recognise is often the initial of their name. At this stage, children may write pages of patterns and symbols, including some of the letters that they know. Often the writing is not intended to carry a meaning.

Lily has produced a piece of writing (below) that shows that she can write her name and contains a mixture of other letters, repeated patterns and streamers.

Lily, aged 3 years and 11 months, shows that she knows some letters and can write her name

Understanding that writing carries a meaning

In the previous stage children were exploring for the satisfaction of discovering interesting things about writing. The next big step is when it becomes obvious that children know that print carries a message. It may be that they can be seen making a shopping list as part of their imaginative play in the home area, or they may attempt to fill in cheques and forms at the post office.

Asking others to read the writing

Towards the end of their fourth year children will produce writing similar to Lily's and will ask adults to read the writing to them. They recognise that writing carries a message and also recognise that they can't read it yet. A little later, when children are nearly 5, they will produce some writing consisting of repeated letters and patterns and will be able to read it out to you. The message may bear no relation to the letters and patterns that have been written, but the children know what they intend the message to say.

Knowing that messages need words

When children begin to write messages, they use what they know about language to help them. They often start with names and know that each name is written differently. They will use the letters they know how to write to produce their own version of names or words. They will use the same 'spelling' consistently in their writing.

Next steps

Children gradually use more conventional spellings by using a variety of strategies. Once children begin to have an understanding of phonics, they can incorporate this into their writing by spelling words as they sound. Children also remember the way a word looks when they have come across it before. The meaning of a word may also help them in their writing.

Methods of helping children write

There are two main ways to helping children learn to write:

- the traditional approach
- the developmental approach.

The traditional approach

This is based on the idea that children enter school with no knowledge about writing and that they can only learn by being given formal instruction from the teacher. In the beginning stages children spend time tracing over teacher's writing, copying teacher's writing and copying from the board. Only after this are children asked to write independently. Writing is done in a book which is later corrected by the teacher.

This method is familiar to many of us but has disadvantages:

- Copying encourages children to be reliant on teachers because children often have to wait for the teacher to supply the word they need.
- There is no emphasis on producing well-constructed, interesting and exciting pieces of writing. Children learn that what their work looks like is more important than the content.

- Children may develop poor attitudes towards writing, becoming discouraged if they feel that they cannot spell or their writing isn't neat.

The developmental approach

In this approach children are seen as active learners. Children actively seek out experiences so that they can learn by experimenting and discovery. This is true for all aspects of children's learning, not just learning to write. By the time children come to school they already know a great deal about writing and the adults' role is to take account of what the children know and support them in their explorations. From the start, children are expected to have a go at writing without waiting for the teacher to give them the correct spelling.

Children are encouraged to think about the meaning of what they are writing and the teacher helps them revise and extend their writing so they find the best way of putting their ideas down. After the writing has been produced the teacher gives feedback about correct letter formation and spelling. The emphasis is on writing for a purpose, rather than routine copying.

This method depends on teachers having an understanding of how writing develops so that they can look at a child's work and know the best way to intervene and help the child move onto the next stage.

It is common practice for the developmental model to be used in nursery classes and other under-5 establishments. Once children enter statutory schooling more teacher-led methods are often used, although some schools will use the developmental approach throughout the primary years. It is rare for any one method to be used exclusively, often a teacher will use elements from both in an effort to meet the needs of individual children in the class. In addition there are published schemes that aim to help develop both reading and writing skills of children that can be used, for example, the Letterland scheme.

Helping children under 5 write

Before considering how to help children write, child-care practitioners must ensure that the children are receiving all-round quality care so that they are able to learn efficiently. Children who are unwell or emotionally insecure will not learn well, even if the best of curriculum resources are provided.

The role of the adult

We have seen that in the developmental model the role of the adult is to take account of what children already know about writing and to facilitate the child in their explorations. Ann Browne (1993) considers that there are four aspects to the adult's role:

- providing the resources that the children need when they write
- acting as a role model by discussing what they are doing and introducing the children to all the purposes of writing in the nursery
- advising children in their writing, encouraging them to have a go, helping them focus on what letters look like, correctly transcribing a child's writing and discussing it with them. This will be done in a spirit of praise and encouragement so children become confident in their developing skills.

- observing the children as they write, monitoring their work and considering how and when to intervene to support the child's progress. Collecting examples of the children's work at regular intervals will help in this.

The writing area

This should be a separate area in the nursery, with imaginative use of dividers so that children are not distracted by others and the area is not part of a thoroughfare within the nursery. Children working in the area should be visible to the adults in the room at all times. The area should be large enough to let several children work at once, with space for an adult to work with them when necessary. The area should be attractive and well resourced so that the children are motivated to use it. The writing area should include the following:

- a variety of paper in different sizes, shapes, colours and quality, including scrap paper
- card
- coupons and forms to fill in
- envelopes
- postcards and greeting cards – they should represent a variety of festivals and should include a variety of languages
- note and message pads
- ready-made booklets of different sizes
- in and out trays
- felt-tip pens, ball-point pens, pencils, crayons, a stapler, a hole punch, rubber stamps, non-toxic glue, labels, pencil sharpener, sticky tape, string, paper clips, ring binders, children's scissors, rulers
- old diaries and calendars
- Letraset, stencils
- a waste bin
- reference materials, such as alphabet books
- a post box which can be emptied at the end of the day
- a word processor.

The writing area should incorporate a display area which not only displays children's work, but also displays writing in other languages, scripts and handwriting styles. Letters and messages that have been received by the class and writing from home can also be displayed.

The nursery staff need to be aware of how the children are using the area and need to suggest new ways of using the resources from time to time. The resources need to be changed regularly to maintain the children's interest and the children need to be encouraged to discuss their work and share it with others.

Visits and visitors

It is important for young children to understand as many different purposes of writing as possible. In the section for the under 3s it was suggested that children should be taken to a variety of places to see people writing in the 'real world'. In the nursery groups of children could be taken out, by prior arrangement, to see hairdressers, doctors' surgeries, hospital outpatients, the police station and the fire station. Quite apart from the value of children learning about adults' work, these visits provide ideal opportunities to see a variety of purposes for writing. It is particularly useful if boys can see men using writing as part of their work. Often boys appear more reluctant than girls to spend time writing. If boys see male fire officers or a male police officers writing this will be a good role model. Conversely girls may get the opportunity to see women police officers and women fire officers in active, powerful positions. It is often possible to arrange for police officers or a fire engine to visit the nursery and they may be able to show the children some of the writing they need to do as part of their work.

Boys and writing

There is concern that boys are falling behind girls in the achievement of literacy skills, both in reading and writing. The differences can be observed as early as the pre-school years and are still there at GCSE level. Although it is wrong to stereotype boys' behaviour, child-care professionals are aware of differences in the way boys play and in their interests. In the pre-school years boys tend to prefer vigorous outdoor play and large construction activities to activities around the graphics table or those which concentrate on small motor skills. Boys, generally show different interests from girls, which is reflected in the games they play and the books that attract them.

It is important to plan writing activities that take account of the boys' interests. The role play area could occasionally be set up as a garage, with log

Writing activities should take account of boys' interests

Over a period of time, observe the different activity areas within the nursery. Using a time sample method (see page 20), record the number of boys and girls every 15 minutes who are playing in the activity area during the course of a day. At the end of the day see if you can identify whether there is a difference in the proportion of boys and girls using the area. If you find differences, suggest ways in which staff could encourage children to participate.

books to write in, appointment books and instruction manuals available. When choosing books to read, choose a mixture of fact and fiction books. If children bring in books from home about the latest cartoon craze, consider reading it to the whole class, after previewing it first to make sure that it is not too aggressive! Boys need to see men writing as part of their jobs and if there are no men working in the nursery then visitors could be invited in or trips arranged where boys can have this experience.

Role-play

Children of this age enjoy role-play and it is customary to have part of the nursery environment set up for this type of activity. Role-play activities can be organised to support children's writing in the same way as for other aspects of the curriculum. The role-play area of the nursery can be set up to correspond to the current theme, or it can be set up as a response to a visit.

The home area can also be organised for children to experiment with writing. There should be the kinds of writing materials that might be found at home, such as pens, pencils, greetings cards and note pads. There can be diaries, calendars, address books and account books. There could be a wipe-clean chart in the kitchen area to put down items to remember for the shopping list. Children can be encouraged to write notes to the person who delivers the milk, label jars in the kitchen and take telephone messages. In addition there needs to be a selection of printed material that you might find in a home, such as magazines, telephone directories, recipe books and newspapers. A tea party can be a good stimulus for writing. There are lists to be made of who to invite, and food to be bought. There are invitations to send out and place names to write.

CASE STUDY

How role-play can provide opportunities for writing

One pre-school group visited a local main Post Office. They looked behind the scenes and saw the postal workers sorting the letters and parcels. One of the staff explained how the letters were delivered from house to house and most of the children were familiar with visits from the postal worker at home. In the front of the building they saw the Post Office staff deal with the public as they bought stamps, paid bills and posted parcels.

When they got back, the staff and children, helped by some parents, set up an area as a post office. They had an area where children could write letters and pack parcels. There were also forms that the Post Office had given them to fill in. There was a counter where 'customers' could buy stamps and hand in forms and parcels for posting. There was also a posting box for the letters. Behind the counter children collected the letters from the box and 'recorded' each one by making marks on a form. Then children took it in turns to deliver the letters.

Opposite is one of the forms that the children used to record the letters that had been posted. At the bottom it looks as if two children have added their signatures. As you can see the 'form' has been made from scrap paper – in role-play props and resources don't have to be completely realistic.

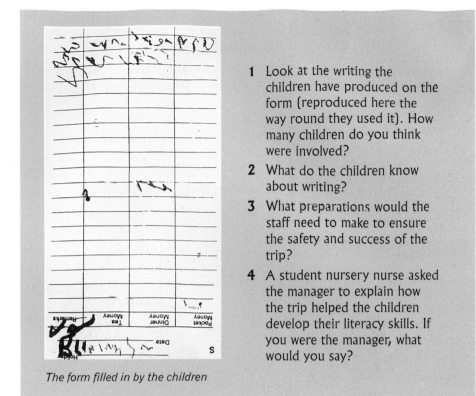

The form filled in by the children

1 Look at the writing the children have produced on the form (reproduced here the way round they used it). How many children do you think were involved?

2 What do the children know about writing?

3 What preparations would the staff need to make to ensure the safety and success of the trip?

4 A student nursery nurse asked the manager to explain how the trip helped the children develop their literacy skills. If you were the manager, what would you say?

THINK ABOUT IT

Write a list of all the activities that can be provided for children to help them develop their fine motor skills.

Other ways of helping the 3–5s

- Make books from pictures that children have drawn as a result of an experience such as a visit.

- Let children see staff members writing. Discuss what you are doing and the purpose of the writing.

- Let children help you make lists and take the register.

- Incorporate writing into other areas of the curriculum, for instance a cooking activity may involve writing out a list of ingredients.

- Use every opportunity for the children to send letters and cards, using their emergent writing skills, to each other, family members, thank you letters to visitors, etc.

- Put an alphabet frieze up in the nursery.

- Plan to include lots of opportunities for children to develop their fine motor skills. Activities may include cutting and sticking, model-making and using material such as dough and clay. Bathing the dolls provides opportunities to do up buttons, hooks and eyes and zips. Small construction helps develop fine motor skills as does playing with jigsaw puzzles.

DO THIS!

1 Look at the example of Lily's writing on page 111. Lily was not quite 4 when she produced this piece of writing. How do you think she is doing compared with other children of her age?

2 Explain why it is not sensible to make a general conclusion about Lily's level of intelligence based on just one piece of evidence.

DEFINITIONS

narrative form the style of writing used to tell a story. This is different from the style used when writing a report or an instruction sheet (non-narrative form)

monosyllabic words words which contain only one syllable, such as **cat**. Words with more than one syllable are known as **polysyllabic**

THINK ABOUT IT

Look at the what children are expected to be able to do at the end of Year 2. Identify the items that could be described as transcription and the items that could be described as composition. You may find the definitions on page 103 helpful.

DEVELOPING WRITING SKILLS IN THE 5–7S

Baseline assessment

In the first term that they are in statutory education children's progress towards learning to write will be assessed. At this age, nearly all children will be able to distinguish between print and pictures in their own work. Many children of this age will be able to write some letter shapes and their own name and a few children will be able to write some words spontaneously.

The National Curriculum

When children enter compulsory education, what they are taught is guided by the National Curriculum and there are expectations about children's achievements at certain ages. Government guidelines on the requirements of the National Curriculum change from time to time and child-care practitioners must make sure that they are aware of current directives.

By the time that children are at the end of Year 2, usually aged 7, they should be able to write well enough to communicate their ideas using both **narrative** and non-narrative forms. Children are expected to be able to use appropriate and interesting vocabulary, and show some awareness of the reader. For instance, the style of a letter to a friend should be different from a report about an activity meant for a newsletter to parents. Children should be able to use sentences, capital letters and full stops. Simple, **monosyllabic words** should be spelt correctly most of the time and where there are inaccuracies the alternative should be phonetically plausible. In their handwriting, children of this age should be able to form letters accurately and letters should be of a consistent size.

The Literacy Hour

The teaching of writing is one of the components of the Literacy Hour in schools, and reflects the importance placed on children being able to write independently from an early stage. There are guidelines and recommendations concerning the implementation of the Literacy Hour and child-care practitioners need to be aware of these. It is recommended that spelling and handwriting are taught in a systematic way so that children can pick up accuracy and speed. Guidelines suggest that children are taught correct letter formation from the outset so that errors are picked up and corrected early on so that they do not hamper children's progress.

Handwriting

Children should develop handwriting that is legible (easy to read), **fluent** and has a reasonable speed. This may seem self-evident but in colleges all round the country we see adult students whose handwriting is neither legible, fluent nor fast. Some students are still at the stage of using print which obviously slows them down. These students are at a considerable disadvantage when it comes to progressing on a course, especially if there is a written exam paper as part of the assessment process.

DEFINITION

fluent   handwriting that the writer finds comfortable to produce. There is a comfortable grip of the pen, the body is relaxed and the letters are formed correctly

Left-handed writers

About 10 per cent of children are left-handed. These children may find difficulties with handwriting. Many children with dyslexia are left-handed, although this is not to say that all left-handed children will have problems with literacy.

The following points have been suggested by Ann Browne to help children who write with their left hand:

- Children need to sit where the light does not cast a shadow of their hand over their writing. Ideally the light should come over their right shoulder.

- Left-handed children need to have the paper placed on the left side of the centre of the body, tilted to the right so that they can see what they are writing.

- If left-handed children are encouraged to hold the pen or pencil further up the shaft than usual, they will be able to see what they are writing.

- Sit left-handed writers far enough away from a right-handed child so that they do not collide when writing.

- Left-handed writers will take longer to develop fast writing than children who are right-handed and allowances should be made for this.

- Demonstrate writing with your left hand as much as possible.

DEFINITIONS

infant print   the first style of writing taught to children – letters are printed in the lower case with capitals for the beginning of sentences and names

cursive script   writing where the individual letters in each word are joined to each other

Handwriting style

Most children learn how to print first, using lower case letters. Capitals are used where appropriate. This kind of writing is often called **infant print**. It is only when children are older that they taught to use 'joined up writing'. However there is a debate as to whether it might be better to introduce children to 'joined up' (**cursive script**) from the beginning.

The advantages of teaching cursive script from the beginning are that:

- children know what they are aiming for from the start of their career
- some researchers view cursive writing as a natural progression from infant 'streamers'
- some researchers consider cursive script to be an aid to spelling.

The advantages of teaching infant print at the beginning are that:

- in emergent writing children appear to go through stages where they start writing capitals, progress to a mixture of capitals and lower case and then to using lower case with appropriate use of capitals. To go from infant scribble straight to cursive script would leave out these 'natural' stages
- the words that children see in books is print, not cursive. Children's first experience of writing is usually print.

On page 120 are two examples of Millicent's writing at the stage when she is beginning to experiment with cursive writing. In the first example you can see that some of her letters have tails on them (sometimes known as exit strokes) – this is a stage before the letters are joined. At least one word (*at*) is joined. In the second example, written only a few weeks later, we can see that Millicent is using cursive script most of the time. Her writing shows another feature that is common at this age – it has become very small.

Millicent, aged 7, is just beginning to experiment with cursive script

A few weeks later, Millicent has used cursive script most of the time

It is important that throughout a school the same way of writing is taught in each class. It is also important that parents and helpers are made aware of policy decisions so that children are provided with a unified approach.

How adults can help with handwriting

- Have a range of writing materials available (see section on helping the under-5s).

- Encourage first drafts to be written in pencil, with pens or felt-tips for second drafts.

- Start young children off with unlined paper. When they start to produce smaller letters and to form them correctly, line guides underneath plain paper, can be introduced. This gives children the freedom to insert drawings where they want too.

- Consider providing alphabet strips that the child can place on their desk when writing, in addition to having an alphabet frieze on the wall.

- Activities from other curriculum areas contribute to handwriting skills, such as art activities, activities that encourage hand–eye co-ordination and the development of fine motor skills.

- Use all areas of the curriculum to provide opportunities for writing.

- Handwriting skills can be taught individually by observing a child writing and offering teaching on letter formation or pencil grip based on what the child has produced. Some authorities consider that handwriting practice should be purposeful in that the child has an audience in mind when he is writing and is prepared to draft and redraft a piece of work so that he can be proud of it.

- Never give the impression that the content is less important than the quality of the handwriting.

- Adults should always be a positive role model and use well formed, clear writing.

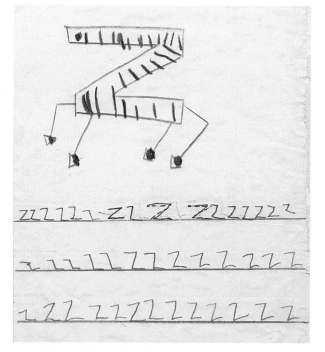

This is a page from 5-year-old Emma's Letterland book

- Some schools use a more formal approach to the teaching of handwriting, where individual letters are practised. There are published schemes available for the teaching of reading and writing. One popular scheme is Letterland.

Spelling

Just as children go through stages in learning to read and write, they also go through stages in learning to spell. In fact all three processes are closely linked. The stages are as follows:

1 At first a child imitates writing and will produce work which contains letter-like shapes, but these letters do not relate to sounds. The example of writing on page 111 shows this clearly.
2 The next stage is when the child is becoming aware of the sounds of letters and uses letter names to represent words. For instance, he might draw a picture of a bee and write the letter *b*.
3 In the third stage a child shows that he understands how to spell words phonetically. He may spell *some* as *sum* or *trouble* as *trubl*.
4 In the final stage the child uses other strategies as well as phonics to help him spell. He uses his knowledge about what a word looks like and his growing awareness of the 'rules' of spelling and the exceptions to these rules.

GOOD PRACTICE

To become good at spelling children must move from a purely phonetic way of spelling towards using a range of strategies.

- Have examples of print around the classroom and draw the children's attention to the shape of words.
- Help the children look for particular letter combinations in words. This encourages visual processing.
- Show the children how complex words can be broken down into smaller ones that they know, such as **armour** into **arm-our**.
- Help children learn families of words, such as **tray, lay** and **day**.
- Instead of giving lists of random words for children to learn to spell, it is more appropriate to take words from children's writing that they have identified as causing them trouble, or that you see are misspelled.
- Do not over-correct a child's work. He may get the impression that the content is not important.
- Teach children the 'look, cover, remember, write and check' method of learning words. In this method the adult writes the word for the child and together they look for patterns, words within words, or other features that will help the child remember the spelling. The child is asked to memorise the word and the word is then covered up. The child writes the word and checks it

against the original version. If the spelling is correct the child goes on to the next spelling. If it is incorrect the child and the adult try to find out where the problem is. The child memorises the word again, covers it and has another attempt at writing it. Only a few words should be learned at a time and the child's recall should be tested after two days and five days, with the process being repeated for words that are misspelled. If the child can remember the spellings after five days they are usually fixed for life. This method has been found much better than just getting children to copy out spellings a number of times.

- Encourage children to draft and redraft their work. Spellings can be corrected in the second draft. Encourage children to proofread their work and try to identify mistakes. Children can work in pairs for this activity. Sentence construction and content can also be reviewed in the second draft.
- Introduce children to dictionaries as soon as possible. They will need to know the alphabet for this and will need teaching in how to use a dictionary efficiently.
- Adults must ensure that they are positive role models and should be seen to check their own spelling.
- Children can be encouraged to develop their own word book.

THINK ABOUT IT

How are computers used as an aid to communication in homes, schools and businesses?

Using computers

It is important that all children are given the opportunity to develop computer skills. Computers can be used to enhance children's learning in all areas of the curriculum, but have a particular relevance when they are learning to write.

For the activity above you probably thought about the use of word-processors, e-mail and the Internet as examples of the use of computers to help us communicate. In many workplaces, the use of computers has replaced writing by hand completely and most of us find ourselves using computers more and more.

It is important that all children are given the opportunity to develop computer skills

The value of introducing children to computers

- Children will learn skills that they will need as they progress through the school system, and in adult life.

- Word-processing a piece of work lets children concentrate on content and communicating ideas.

- Word-processing encourages children to draft and redraft their work, allowing them to correct spelling and sentence construction easily. These skills can then be used in drafting and redrafting their handwritten work.

- Writing that is word-processed looks very professional when mounted and displayed. Children feel that their work is valued.

- Word-processing encourages children to branch out into different styles of writing, for instance writing for a newsletter, writing 'business' letters to organisations and writing reports.

- For children who are dyslexic or who find writing by hand physically difficult, word-processing is liberating. Voice recognition packages can be very useful.

- The Internet and the use of e-mail can be used to gather information and communicate with other schools and organisations.
- There are many computer packages designed to help children with all aspects of the curriculum, including improving literacy skills.

✔ PROGRESS CHECK

1 What is the difference between infant print and cursive script?

2 What are the arguments for and against the introduction of infant print when children are learning to write?

3 Describe the stages in learning to spell.

4 What is the best way to help children learn a list of spellings?

KEY TERMS

You need to know the meaning of the following words and phrases. Go back through the chapter to make sure you understand them:

composition
cursive script
developmental writing
emergent writing
fluent
infant print
inferior pincer grip or grasp
monosyllabic form
narrative form
palmar grasp
pincer grip or grasp
preferred hand
transcription
tripod grip or grasp

FURTHER READING

Browne, A. (1993) *Helping Children to Write*, Paul Chapman
This is a practical book, full of useful suggestions and is suitable for practitioners and students on level three and four courses.

Clay, M. (1987) *Writing Begins at Home*, Heinemann
This book will be an invaluable resource for anyone working with children of pre-school age. The text is very accessible and the book is full of examples of children's writing. It is suitable for students on child-care courses at all levels.

Whitehead, M. (1996) *The Development of Language and Literacy*, Hodder & Stoughton
This book has a useful section on helping children develop their writing skills.

Whitehead, M. (1999) *Supporting Language and Literacy Development in the Early Years*, Open University Press
This book is useful because it contains a chapter that looks at good practice in the provision for language and literacy in two early years settings.

Bilingualism

The key topics covered in this chapter are:

- Definitions of bilingualism
- Attitudes to bilingualism
- Bilingualism and intelligence
- Bilingualism and education
- Helping young children to learn a second language.

Think about the bilingual children you have known in nurseries/schools or in your family. In which ways did being bilingual benefit them? Were there any ways in which they were disadvantaged? If you are bilingual yourself, spend some time thinking about how you felt about being bilingual as a child.

As our understanding of how children acquire language has evolved so has our awareness of the effects bilingualism has on young children who are both acquiring language and entering an educational system. Political approaches, societal and cultural attitudes, ignorance of the benefits of bilingualism and a general lack of understanding and resources have tended towards bilingualism being viewed as a problem, at least in educational terms. Bilingualism should be a positive aspect of any child's or adult's life. This is ensured when language and cultural diversity are valued and celebrated. Unless otherwise stated in this chapter the term bilingualism also includes multilingualism.

DEFINITIONS OF BILINGUALISM

Defining bilingualism

There are many definitions of bilingualism. Producing an accurate definition is interesting and complex. It concerns such questions as proficiency, how the languages a speaker has are used and how the person using them switches between one language and another. In everyday usage, a **bilingual** person is considered to be someone who speaks two languages. A multilingual person

DO THIS!

Write your own definition of bilingualism in two or three sentences. If your are working in a group, compare your definition with those of other members of the group.

Compare your definition with the definitions that follow later in this section.

DEFINITIONS

bilingual literally, two languages – in everyday use, a bilingual person is someone who speaks two languages; it refers to people who have access to a second linguistic code, but do not necessarily have full skills of listening, reading, speaking and writing in either language

balanced bilingual a person who can listen, speak, read and write with equal proficiency in two languages

monolingual a person who knows and uses only one language

linguistic code a term used instead of the word language to describe a language being used in a community

THINK ABOUT IT

Language is a unique and very individual skill involving many aspects of a human being – speaking, listening, reading, writing, cultural background and complex emotional attitudes. Consider whether there can be such a thing as a balanced bilingual.

can speak three or more languages. Equal fluency is often assumed, though it is common for bilingual speakers, even those who have been bilingual from birth to be somewhat dominant in one of the languages.

Definitions of bilingualism, particularly those used for educational or scientific purposes tend to be concerned with measurement and/or content of the second language. Suzanne Romaine (1994) lists four skills that ought to be present when assessing the degree of bilingualism:

- listening
- reading
- speaking
- writing.

A person who can use all four skills equally in both languages is described as a **balanced bilingual**. This description is not an ideal one as it is very difficult to measure language skills even in **monolingual** people. The term 'bilingual' in everyday use tends to include those who have access to a second **linguistic code**, but do not have all four skills in either their first or second languages. Usually a person who has considerable proficiency in reading, comprehension and writing but is very poor in understanding or using oral language is not considered a bilingual. It is difficult to measure the language skills of any person and in research situations the language skills of each individual taking part is given a score so that comparisons can be made but this method of measurement usually ignores the social context of language.

Some definitions of bilingualism

The following definitions of bilingual have been used:

- 'a person who knows and uses two languages' (*Dictionary of Language Teaching and Applied Linguistics*, Longman, 1997)
- 'able to speak two languages fluently' (*The Oxford English Reference Dictionary*, 1996)
- 'native-like control of two languages' (L. Bloomfield, *Language*, New York: Holt, 1933)
- 'the psychological state of an individual who has access to one or more linguistic codes as a means of social communication' (J.F. Hamers and M.H. Blanc, *Bilingualcy and Bilingualism*, Cambridge University Press, 1989).

The following terms are used to give a more accurate picture of bilingualism:

- *balanced bilingual* – a person who speaks, reads, writes and understands two languages equally well
- *dominant bilingual* – a person who is more proficient in one of the two languages
- *transitional bilingual* – usually refers to a child in school or nursery whose first language is being partly used to make transfer to the school language easier

THINK ABOUT IT

Which of the above definitions of bilingualism do you consider to be the most appropriate? Give as many reasons as possible for your choice.

DEFINITIONS

native speaker   a speaker of a language acquired in early childhood because it is spoken in the family and it is the language of the country where the person lives

heritage language   the language which has been passed on from generation to generation in the cultural group to which the child belongs; usually spoken at home by a child's parents; also referred to as **home language**

- *passive bilingual* – a person who is a **native speaker** of one language and is able to understand but not speak a second language; such a person may also be called a *receptive bilingual*

- *simultaneous bilingual* – both languages are learned as first languages, as in the case of infants who are exposed to two languages from birth.

How definitions are used

Definitions of bilingualism are used to fit particular situations. For example a child in a nursery or primary school is described as being bilingual if the language used at home is different from that used in school. The child may be fluent in her **home language** but may not yet have acquired more than a minimum vocabulary in the school language. Likewise a child may be able to speak, read, write and listen age-appropriately at school but may only be able to speak and listen in the **heritage language**.

For research using bilingual adults or children an accurate definition of bilingualism is essential so that accurate comparisons can be made. Many of the bilingual people used to research language have been balanced bilinguals.

✔ PROGRESS CHECK

1 When the term bilingual is used in everyday language, what does it mean?
2 What does multilingual mean?
3 If you wanted to give a precise definition of bilingual, what would you have to take into account?
4 There are four skills which a balanced bilingual should have in each language. What are they?
5 What does transitional bilingualism mean?

ATTITUDES TO BILINGUALISM

The importance of attitudes

An attitude is an internal, emotional way of viewing something, which might explain the actions of a person. Attitudes to language are something which individuals or groups may possess which are likely to promote certain behaviours as well as determine the status of a language. Where attitudes are positive, they promote positive effects; where negative, harm can result. Attitudes to bilingualism are complex and vary from person to person. They are often informed by historical perspectives on language in a particular place, by societal prejudice towards a cultural group or by knowledge acquired by direct contact with the speakers of a certain language. Attitudes are usually modified by experience. Positive or negative attitudes towards the home language of a young bilingual child can determine the overall educational experience which the child will have. People from minority groups will sometimes have negative attitudes towards their own language because they may not see it as a means of 'getting on' in the wider community. People are also subtly influenced by an **institutional disregard** for any language other than the dominant one.

'No, don't use Cantonese. Say "Yes, please" or you can't have any.'

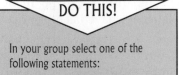

In your group select one of the following statements:

- Nursery worker, herself bilingual in English and Cantonese, to a child at the snack table:

  'Do you want another biscuit? No, don't use Cantonese. Say "Yes, please" or you can't have any more biscuits.'

- One child to another who was using English to a Turkish-speaking child: 'He's not able to talk.'

- 'If I go to another country I don't expect them all to speak English to me. Why can't those who come here get down to learning English and then we wouldn't have all this fuss?'

Make a list of, and then discuss, the values and assumptions of the speakers.

Historical perspectives

From the beginning of recorded history people have traversed the world. Sometimes this was to find a better place to live. At other times it was with the express purpose of forcefully taking over new territory and subduing the population in that place. As people travelled so did their languages. Their languages usually helped to preserve their identity but as time passed these languages would become subsumed into the dominant language and were then often completely wiped out. If the newcomers had forcibly taken over territories, they often set about wiping out the language of that place as a means of further subduing the conquered people. Recent examples of this were the forceful displacement of Gaelic in Scotland, Irish in Ireland and Welsh in Wales in favour of the English language. Historical linguists have been able to show where this has happened in the more distant past.

One way of displacing a minority language is through the medium of education. Despite the linguistic diversity in the world, educational systems until the latter half of the twentieth century have been largely monolingual. In Europe this dates back to the Greek and Roman Empires where Greek and Latin were used and the many local languages ignored. There were changes in the eighteenth and nineteenth centuries when **ethnolinguistic groups** throughout the world began to organise their own schools, but this process was halted at about the beginning of the twentieth century, when monolingual education became the norm as the result of the growth of universal public education. However, a small number of European countries did manage to keep more than one of the languages spoken within their borders represented in their educational systems.

In 1951, UNESCO (United Nations Educational and Scientific Organisation) considered the question of language for education on a worldwide basis and concluded that the most important factor was the well-being of individual children. They suggested that the child's '**mother tongue**' should be used at the beginning of a child's education and for as long as possible thereafter. In Britain this idea took some decades to become part of the general thinking. Implementation took much longer and it was and still is hampered by a lack of financial resources. The Bullock Report, *A Language for Life*, published in 1975, was the first report to indicate that many children from ethnic minority groups did not achieve at school because their heritage cultures and language were largely ignored. The report stated that: 'No child should be expected to cast off the language and culture of home as he crosses the school threshold, and the curriculum should reflect those aspects of his life.'

By the 1980s it was accepted that children speaking a language other than English when they arrive at school need to have their home language respected and encouraged in order to facilitate their overall language development and learning.

> ### DEFINITION
>
> **mother tongue**   the first language which is acquired at home; the terms heritage language or home language are now more widely used

Effects of early research

Much of the research carried out in the first half of the twentieth century found results which indicated that bilingual speakers had a lower level of IQ. This was done mainly in America in the 1920s on immigrants from Eastern Europe who spoke a variety of languages and who were often fleeing from persecution. They were not able to cope very well with the type of tests that were presented to them in unfamiliar circumstances.

In Wales, at about the same time, similar results were found though the difference seemed to be between urban and rural children. Rural children had possibly less exposure to English – the language in which the tests were administered. The effects of the results of these studies lasted well into the 1980s and have affected the way parents and educators have viewed the maintenance and acquisition of second or other languages. Some of the myths about bilingualism which we look at in the next section are the results of this thinking. One of the reasons why the research undertaken then produced results which resulted in negative attitudes towards bilingualism was because we now know that there were difficulties inherent in intelligence testing. These were mainly a lack of understanding about how people in certain situations might respond, for instance, their lack of familiarity with the language in which the tests were administered and the trauma of being in a new situation. The social, political or economic situations at the time may have found negative findings more useful for their purposes and it is now well known that researchers often, though not deliberately, produced results which were influenced by the then current thinking and needs. An example of this occurred in America in the 1920s when the government had to cope with waves of immigrants all seeking work. The thinking was that if the educational system ensured that everyone spoke English then life would be much easier.

DO THIS!

Either:

1 If you work in a culturally diverse nursery or classroom (i.e. where the children come from many different cultures and speak many different languages in their homes), make a list of the ways that the heritage languages of the children are encouraged.
   a) How do you think the children benefit from what is being done?
   b) If there were unlimited resources, what else would be beneficial?

Or:

2 If you work in a setting where almost all the children are monolingual, list any ways in which they are made aware of languages in the wider society.

Current situation

The value of speaking more than one language is now fairly well understood. However, there are still problems in that some languages are not valued because the culture from which they come is not valued. Parents in these situations are concerned that their children are successful and see access to the dominant language as a means of doing this. In the next section we will look at what educators can do to remove such bias.

There is growing awareness, however, of the benefits of bilingualism. As far back as 1986, a US News and World Report stated that according to the Centre for Applied Linguistics in Washington, DC, there were 1,200 language programmes throughout America for children under 6 years to enable them to learn a second language. In Britain and in Ireland there are many out-of-school classes where children are taught a range of languages. Parents are usually the driving force behind such classes. They are aware that exposure to second and even more languages is likely to have intellectual benefits for their children. They are also aware that the world is getting smaller, that there will be a greater need for communication in the future and that their children's intellectual and educational abilities are enhanced by exposure to more than one language. Greater ethnic pride has also encouraged parents to ensure that their children speak, read and write in their heritage language.

Transmission of cultural messages through language

In 1978 Vygotsky was the first psychologist to suggest the importance of the role that language plays in transmitting information about a culture, particularly the culture to which children belong. He used the term 'cultural tools' (see page 6) to describe the symbolic signs we use – speech, reading, writing – which help us and young children to develop a sense of cultural identity and internalise the cultural norms (accept as one's own the 'rules' of behaviour in a culture) and knowledge of our particular culture. Children who are not encouraged to develop their heritage language may be in danger of:

- not internalising knowledge and understanding of their heritage culture
- feeling alienated from those who should be closest to them – parents and extended family
- developing poor self-esteem through not valuing what is their first language and an essential part of themselves
- being deprived of a skill – becoming bilingual – which, it is considered, enhances their intellectual abilities
- not achieving their educational potential
- developing psychological problems in adulthood resulting from a sense of loss.

- Learn as much as possible about the language and culture of the children in your care. Get help from other members of your team, from parents and from reading.
- Where possible, learn some of the key words from the languages used by the children in your nursery or school. Useful words to learn would be words for greeting, as well as lunch and toilet.
- Value language diversity as a rich resource which will enhance the lives of all the children in your care.
- It is important to also value your own language. This will enable you to value other languages.

An educational system (or a society) which does not value the heritage languages of its members does not give positive cultural messages. This may encourage prejudice and resultant problems. In Britain there is a disparity in the way languages are valued. European languages, on the whole, are highly valued, whereas African and Asian languages are not. Rather they are considered a handicap. Thus, the ability to speak French or German is highly prized by many people whereas only a minority of people would consider it beneficial to learn Urdu. Ignorance of culture and tradition has resulted in no educational, political or economic privileges being attached to these languages.

Parents/carers can help us to learn about their language and culture

Myths about bilingualism

Despite the knowledge that has become available about the value of bilingualism, myths (untrue but often widely held beliefs) have persisted which have often resulted in children not being encouraged to develop a second language. In particular, parents who are themselves speakers of minority languages have become fearful of encouraging the use of the home language. Such myths have taken the form of statements like:

- 'Learning two languages confuses a child and affects his intelligence.'
- 'A child should be able to speak one language properly first before he can begin to learn a second one.'
- 'If he learns two languages he won't feel at home in either of them. He will always be between two cultures.'
- 'He will end up with a split personality.'.

These statements are untrue and they are very upsetting for parents/carers who are not fully aware of the value of bilingualism. Child-care practitioners should, where appropriate, help parents and colleagues to become informed about the value of bilingualism.

CASE STUDY

Yusuf

Yusuf was 2 when his Turkish-speaking family moved to England. Yusuf was developing his home language quickly and talked most of his waking hours. He particularly enjoyed books and stories. His only exposure to English was when they went shopping or through television. Yusuf enthusiastically started at the local nursery when he was just 3. There were two other children there who did not speak English at home. The staff firmly believed that it was in the children's best interests to learn English quickly and they put effort into making them give English responses. Though they did not ask Yusuf's mother to speak English to him, they gave her books in English to read to him at home. His parents' English was limited, but they did their best to speak English where possible to him and worried that he was not responding even a little bit. They now rarely read him stories in Turkish and he only occasionally looked at his books. Yusuf became quiet and withdrawn and would scream 'No' when his mother suggested a story in Turkish. Fortunately they had to move home and he started at another nursery where there were many Turkish-speaking children. The children's home languages were encouraged and stories in Turkish were read several times a week. He was back to his old self within a month and happily using quite a considerable vocabulary in English in the nursery as well.

1 Was it a good idea for the staff in the first nursery to give Yusuf's mother English books to read to him at home?

2 Why do you think Yusuf got so upset when his mother suggested reading a story in Turkish?

3 What conditions in the second nursery enabled Yusuf to return to his old self?

✔ PROGRESS CHECK

1 Why are positive attitudes towards heritage languages essential for young children?

2 Why did UNESCO suggest that 'mother tongue' should be used at the beginning of a child's education?

3 Why might children who are not encouraged to develop their heritage language fail to develop a knowledge of their culture?

4 Name two myths about bilingual education which might discourage parents from ensuring that their children are taught a second language?

BILINGUALISM AND INTELLIGENCE

Bilingualism as an aid to intelligence

It is now widely accepted that being bilingual helps general intelligence. Writers and researchers on bilingualism and intelligence generally agree with this. Colin Baker (1988) says that 'Bilingualism is to intelligence as food is to human fitness.' There are a number of reasons, however, why we should be careful about completely accepting this thinking. These are concerned with the difficulties inherent in understanding and measuring intelligence. They are concerned with:

- the nature of intelligence – can we measure something that we cannot directly observe?
- the fact that it is widely accepted that intelligence testing can only measure a small part of what is considered to be intelligence. It does not measure intelligent behaviour, inborn potential as a result of genetic or hereditary influences, nor emotional intelligence. These are not, at the present time, capable of being objectively measured
- the research which measures the intelligence of balanced bilinguals and monolinguals has always tended to ignore the controversies surrounding intelligence and in particular the use of tests to measure intelligence
- in any intelligence testing, the results could be influenced by any previous training which the child might have received, or the experiences which an adult might have been exposed to, might encourage proficiency or a lack of proficiency in such tests
- the other environmental effects which might affect test results – strangeness, sense of security, noise and the type of relationship which might exist between the tester and the child or adult who is being tested.

Advantages of bilingualism

Despite the problems inherent in the measurement of intelligence, it is now widely accepted that being bilingual benefits children. Research now tends to focus more narrowly on specific cognitive skills, for example reading. Bialystok, in her article 'Words as things: Development of word concept by bilingual children' (*Journal of Studies in Second Language Acquisition*, 9, 133–40, 1987), assessed the difference between bilingual and monolingual children's emerging concept of print. She found that bilingual children understood better than monolingual children the general symbolic representation of print they were exposed to. Hakuta, in *Mirror of Language: The Debate on Bilingualism* (New York: Basic Books, 1986), found that pre-school children who can speak two languages learn to read more quickly than their monolingual peers. These findings do not necessarily prove that all children benefit from being bilingual. However, despite the difficulties mentioned in the last section about intelligence testing in general, a review of the research would appear to indicate that the advantages of bilingualism for children would appear to be:

- *cognitive*, i.e. relating to a range of abstract skills – thinking, reasoning, understanding, problem-solving and many others
- *emotional* (generally relating to states such as happiness, sadness, grief, etc.) and *social*.

Cognitive advantages
- Bilingualism has been shown to increase children's understanding of concepts. Having different words for an object increases general under-

standing. Bilingual children have also been shown to be more imaginative and better with abstract notions (ideas and thoughts about concepts that are unrelated to actual objects and events).

- Research has shown that children who are bilingual have better symbolic representation so they have less difficulty learning to read.
- Children develop **metalinguistic skills** and are better able to reflect on language.
- Having access to two languages encourages **divergent thinking**, thus logical reasoning is developed.
- Language transmits a knowledge and understanding of the culture to which the language belongs.
- An appreciation of the richness of language and culture is developed.
- The flexibility in thinking which bilingualism develops is transferred to other areas of learning.

Emotional/social advantages

- If a child is in an environment where being able to speak a second language is valued, self-esteem and confidence is developed.
- Further language learning is made easier because children are not inhibited by making new strange sounds.
- Knowledge of a heritage language is likely to bring about closer family relationships.
- Sensitivity to the nuances of language is developed and the child is thus better able to assess situations.

> **DEFINITIONS**
>
> **metalinguistic skills** being able to think about what language is for and how it is used
>
> **divergent thinking** being able to think in different ways about something

Knowledge of a heritage language is likely to bring about closer family relationships

BILINGUALISM AND EDUCATION

Different types of bilingual education

There are a variety of types of bilingual education. The term 'bilingual education' suggests that it is education where two languages are used within a school. This is not strictly correct as only one language within the school may be used for instruction and communication but it may not be the language used by the children at home or in the community. Examples of this type of bilingual education are Welsh-speaking schools in Wales and the Gaelscoileanna in Ireland, which are immersion models of bilingual education (see page 136).

Kreher and Wong were quoted in a review of their article on global multlingualism (*Language and Society*, 25, 1996) as saying that 'There can be no general theory of bilingual education. Individual linguistic and socio-economic factors matter more than educational methodology, so that the same education strategy which may result in success in one place may result in failure in another.' It is therefore important for any individual or institution promoting or delivering bilingual education to be able to clearly answer the following questions:

- Is it always the best idea to teach a child through the medium of her heritage language?
- Which is best for a child – to be exposed to instruction through the dominant language or through the second language which is less likely to develop?
- Are there socio-economic reasons in this particular situation why a child might achieve poorly in school?
- What are the social and political assumptions about the value of bilingualism in this particular situation?
- Will support from the wider community be positive and if not how can the situation be dealt with?

DO THIS!

Either:

1 If you are familiar with a situation where many local languages are the normal school or nursery situation, discuss these questions with your group.

Or:

2 You may be unfamiliar with such a situation. If so, discuss with your group your understanding of these questions.

Transitional bilingual education

Transitional bilingual education is considered to be 'the partial or total use of the child's home language when the child enters school, and at a later stage the use of the school language only' (*Dictionary of Language Teaching and Applied Linguistics*, Longman, 1997). The overall plan here is to phase out the home language as the school language develops. This is really not bilingual education but a monolingual approach. It is an interim measure which may enable the child to:

- settle more quickly at school
- continue to develop and lay down the structures of her first language which is considered very important for overall language learning
- benefit from the value attached to her heritage language and culture.

In many schools and nurseries this takes the form of staff learning some basic words in the child's language, employing bilingual classroom assistants, having bilingual teachers who can visit a class for a period of time each day and providing a variety of resources like tapes and books in the child's language. Parents are encouraged to talk and read to the child in the home language and occasionally siblings and other older children are encouraged to help. The intellectual gains from bilingualism are not a particular feature of this system, but it is intended that by aiding the development of the first language the learning of a second language will be made easier. It is also assumed that where the language and culture of a child is valued there will be gains in self-esteem which will aid general learning. However, such a system would be financially impossible where there are many different languages.

Immersion programmes

Children on these programmes are 'immersed' in the chosen second language. Just as children learn their native language by being exposed to it in a non-pressurised way when they are very young, so children on immersion programmes learn a second language. In such schools the language of instruction and communication between children staff and management is the second language. Usually the children start at school (or pre-school) with very little or no exposure to the second language. All instruction is in the second language from the beginning and teachers and early years practitioners rely heavily on visual aids, body language and gesture to ensure understanding. Children are permitted to use their first language for as long as they find it necessary.

Examples of successful immersion programmes are in Canada where there are two official languages, English and French, and parents want their children to be fluent in both languages. Immersion programmes are becoming increasingly popular in the USA where parents are anxious that their children grow up bilingual, but do not have access to a second language themselves. Spanish immersion programmes are the most popular in the United States but there are many others. In Ireland there are now over 200 Gaelscoileanna where the Irish language is the medium of instruction. In nearly all cases the children who attend these schools are not exposed to the second language either at home or in the wider community. Research has shown that these children do not become bilingual at the expense of the other curriculum areas and in fact they often do as well or better than comparable non-immersion pupils.

The main benefits of such a system are considered to be that children:

- grow up bilingual
- are capable of greater divergent thinking skills
- have improved listening skills
- have enhanced critical thinking skills
- develop an awareness of other cultures.

Cloic no Coilte Gaelscoil in Ireland, where the Irish language is the medium of instruction

Maintenance or enrichment bilingual education

In a maintenance or enrichment programme, the home language is kept throughout the period of schooling. There are examples of this type of education in Wales and Canada where children receive some of their teaching in Welsh or French to enable them to be fully bilingual. A similar model of bilingual education exists in Luxembourg where the entire population becomes trilingual (in Luxemburger, German and French).

Unlike children in an immersion programme, who may have no input from their homes or the community to the language taught at school, children in maintenance programmes are likely to have contact with the second language in the wider community.

DO THIS!

Check your local area to see what language classes are available for young children. If you can talk to somebody in charge of one of these classes, find out what the aims of that particular class is.

Other bilingual programmes

In most countries there are programmes which are set up by communities and some religious groups to enable children to progress in their heritage language or to learn a language for religious reasons. Jewish children often attend Hebrew classes and Muslim children learn Arabic. Such programmes are usually the result of a desire on the part of adults in minority groups to pass on their culture and religion as well as their language to their children. The success of such classes is dependent on the financial resources available, the availability of suitable teachers and the stamina required by both children and parents to give time to an out-of-school activity.

✔ PROGRESS CHECK

1 What is an immersion programme?
2 Explain what transitional bilingualism is.
3 What is a maintenance or enrichment programme?

GOOD PRACTICE

- It is essential to value each child's culture and heritage language.
- Supporting the home language will make it easier for the child to learn a new language.
- Be aware that negative stereotypes are harmful to the child. An example of this would be the view that a child may find it more difficult to learn because she speaks a minority language.
- Remember that children are individuals and will vary in the speed with which they will begin to use the new language. Some children will begin to use words almost immediately; others may need a very long listening time – often six months – before they begin to use the new language.
- It is important to be aware of the child's progress in the home language. If this is proceeding normally there is usually no need to worry about the child's acquisition of the second language.

HELPING YOUNG CHILDREN TO LEARN A SECOND LANGUAGE

The importance of good practice

This section does not deal with an immersion model of bilingual education, although many of the principles used in such settings would have value in any setting where young children enter a school or nursery and have to learn an additional language. In any setting it is important to remember that learning language is only one feature of the child's total experience. Child-care practitioners always need to be aware of the development of the whole child. If they are not, other areas of development may be neglected. Good practice which will benefit all children will be especially beneficial to bilingual children.

Learning a second language

A child who is learning a second language at school needs to be part of that school from the beginning. It is essential that children are not made to feel different by being removed for special classes. Where this is done it should be minimised and its value should be critically assessed. Learning the additional language will be made easier if it is taken into account that:

- Children learn a second language because they want to communicate in that language.
- Language is best taught to children when they are taking part in the normal curriculum activities.
- The language taught must be the same as the language used daily by all the children.
- Plenty of listening time is important.

- It is not a good idea to insist on oral responses too early as this may hinder learning. Accept any response the child makes either in her own language or through gesture or facial expression.

- Activities which are good for helping a child to learn a second language are also good for reinforcing the language learning of monolingual children.

- Children make excellent teachers and helpers.

- Bilingual children should be given opportunities where they can use language with their peers. This can be done making sure they have opportunities to play in both small and large groups.

- It will help the child if the home language is supported as much as resources will allow.

- Bilingualism can be a positive factor in children's intellectual and emotional development.

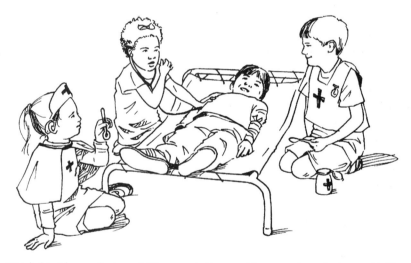

Language is best learned when children are taking part in normal curriculum activities

Helping children to get started with a second or additional language

Early years practitioners need to feel confident about their ability to help children easily acquire a second language. It is also important that they enjoy language diversity themselves. Each nursery or school will have its own guidelines which will need to be regularly reviewed as new information becomes available. Practitioners will have their own understanding of what works well with children learning a second language and their observations should be valued.

GOOD PRACTICE

- Continue talking even when children do not understand.
- Make use of varied questions.
- Remember that what is talked about should be in context. Children need to see what you are talking about.
- Be persistent in including the child in small groups with other children.
- Make other children the focus of conversation.
- Make use of the first language if this is possible and appropriate.
- Accept all non-verbal responses – gestures, facial expressions, eye contact.

- Do not insist on oral responses.
- Praise minimal efforts.
- Structure play to encourage child-to-child interaction.
- Read and tell repetitive stories.
- Have story props of familiar stories available and allow the children to use them themselves.
- Make use of songs, rhymes and simple poems.
- Ensure that the classroom or nursery is calm and welcoming.
- If possible, give the child opportunities in school or nursery where she can also use her home language – in play situations, with visitors and bilingual staff.

DO THIS!

Plan an activity for a small group of three or four children, aged between 3 and 4, one of whom has just started at the nursery and whose home language is not English. Write a rationale for your activity.

Before carrying it out, prepare learning outcomes for the group and for the child learning English.

Keeping records and assessment

Some means of recording children's progress in their new language is essential if they are to be helped to progress further. Children's progress in their home language should also be recorded. This can usually be done with the help of parent and carers. It is also important that the child gets the opportunity of using her home language in the school – in play situations, with other children, with visitors and bilingual staff. Nurseries and schools will have their own methods of recording progress. The checklist opposite may serve as a guide. It is also important to remember that children's progress in language may be in rapid spurts and a discussion on any assessment must ensure that that assessment is up-to-date.

A child's language progress report can usually be undertaken with the help of parents/carers

You may experience difficulty completing some of the tasks set out in the following checklist. If you wish to complete some or all of the checklist on a child in your placement, you must first discuss it with your supervisor and obtain permission from both the parents and the practitioner in charge.

CHECKLIST FOR RECORDING PROGRESS IN A NEW LANGUAGE

Name: ....

	Tick	Comments
Settling in school or nursery: • Does not speak but joins in with activities • Communicates using non-verbal gestures • Indicates that English is being understood • Uses home language quite a lot • Follows very simple instructions but is dependent on gesture • Substitutes words from home language when needed • Uses essential vocabulary		
Getting familiar with English: • Uses English in most situations with peers and adults • Able to construct simple sentences • Uses language to express needs • Shows that a considerable amount of English is understood • Substitutes words from first language where necessary but not so often • Listens attentively in one-to-one situations • Can follow simple instructions • Understands and uses simple vocabulary		
Becoming a confident user of English: • Confidently able to use English in social situations • Sentences have correct order of words • Sentences becoming more complex • Can follow almost all instructions • Listens attentively in small groups		
Able to use additional language fluently: • Confidently uses English with peers and adults • Moves with ease from home language to English • Articulation is clear and easy to understand • Listens attentively in large groups • Uses language to explain, describe, predict, discuss and reason • Able to hold logical conversations of an age-appropriate length • Initiates questions and conversations		

DO THIS!

Use the first two parts of the checklist to assess the progress of a child who is in his or her first year in the nursery. Write an evaluation of the progress of the child and suggest any action that could be taken to enhance the language skills the child has learned.

As already mentioned, you will need appropriate permission before undertaking this task.

The use of resources

The use of resources to enhance the learning of additional languages and for developing cultural awareness have been a feature in British classrooms since the late 1970s. Resources are a valuable aid but they should not be used uncritically. It is important that they are well presented using the best quality materials available and in no way inferior to other resources available in English. The most common examples are:

- dual texts
- books in languages other than English
- materials, such as games, posters and charts
- self-made materials.

Dual texts

Dual texts are books or other resources where the text is written in English and in another language. They are good for promoting linguistic and cultural diversity. Its essential that in any dual-text book that the minority language is not given negative status by being written in smaller text or by being hand-written. Having the English text first on all occasions will give children the impression that the second language is not as important. Children who are reading or beginning to read will usually use the English text. Teachers may need to discuss with bilingual children which language to read first and why, and develop strategies to encourage them to read their community language first. A positive feature of having a range of dual-text books is that they develop language awareness and cultural respect in monolingual children.

Books in languages other than English

These books should be selected carefully. The criteria that governs the selection of all books for young children should also be applied to books in languages other than English. The availability of such books will help all children to develop awareness of languages other than their own and they may also be a useful resource for parents who wish to develop their children's home language.

Materials, such as games, posters and charts

There are now many suppliers of these materials in the UK. They are usually of very good quality. Large firms usually employ native speakers, or reputable translators of the language being used, when designing these materials. Whatever the source – well-known suppliers or from abroad – they should be carefully checked to ensure that they meet acceptable standards. They should be as well-designed and presented as any of the other resources that are available in the setting.

Self-made materials

There are less self-made materials in use now as educational suppliers and publishers are supplying appropriate items. However, it is essential that any of these items use appropriate translations and spelling and avoid the use of handwritten script in the additional language unless appropriate.

Imported materials into Britain occasionally come from the USA and Australia (where there are large minority second language groups), but more often they are from the country of origin. Before using them, you need to consider whether the quality of the paper or the colours used are likely to give negative language status messages to young children. It is important to consider also how the children might view them because the adults' judgement might be culturally influenced. A further consideration might be whether the experiences they portray are far removed from the current situation. In the case of books which the children are likely to read in their home languages, it is necessary to consider whether they are geared for children who have greater competence

You need to be careful that the resources available are not **tokenistic**, to think critically about how best to use them with the children and to observe how they are used by the children, their parents/carers and themselves.

✔ PROGRESS CHECK

1 List some of the ways that a child who has just started in a second language environment can be helped?
2 List four things you can do to help a child learn a second language?
3 Why is it important to know about a child's progress in the home language?
4 Dual-text storybooks and other resources can sometimes give children negative status messages about some languages. What would cause this to happen?

ACCENTS AND DIALECTS

Dialects

Dialect is the name given to the various ways that a country's language is spoken in different regions of that country and sometimes between different social classes. The differences show themselves in accent, pronunciation, grammar and the use of idioms (see page 4). Dialects are sometimes referred to as 'speech varieties' as this is considered a more neutral way of describing language differences. Well-known examples of dialects in the UK are Geordie, Lancashire and Glaswegian. African–Caribbean people in the UK speak a dialect known as Patois (but different Caribbean islands have their own languages and dialects).

Dialects have been spoken in localised communities in the UK for centuries and indeed Standard English, which is considered the 'correct way' to speak English, is just another dialect adopted by the powerful and educated classes. The development of dialects has been part of the evolving and dynamic nature of language. It is important to see them as part of the richness of our culture and to recognise that both their speakers and the dialects themselves need to be valued like any other minority language.

If children's heritage languages and cultures are not valued in school, the children are considered to be disadvantaged. The same is very likely to be true for speakers of certain dialects. It is expected that children entering school will have an understanding of Standard English before they come to school, but this is not automatically the case. Non-standard dialects are not usually given the consideration and additional linguistic status that second languages are given. Further problems arise if speakers of non-standard dialects are stereotyped as being less articulate and intelligent than speakers of Standard English. It is often accepted that speakers of Standard English will have difficulty with accents and dialects but not the other way round.

Children very much need to feel that they belong and if they are speakers of a non-standard dialect, this part of their linguistic and cultural identity needs to be understood and valued.

Accents

Accents refer to the particular way that words are pronounced. Everybody has an accent. An accent might show the region or country or even the first language of a speaker. Examples of accents are Scottish accents, Lancashire accents and French accents. Accents may be part of dialects, but Standard English may also be spoken with a particular accent. They may also indicate the social class of a speaker.

> **DEFINITION**
>
> **stereotypes** over-generalisations about a group or class of people usually based on biased or inaccurate beliefs

Accents may result in the speakers being subject to the same **stereotypical** views that are sometimes held of speakers of a particular dialect. It is therefore important to ensure when dealing with young children that regional or other accents are not seen as any type of indicator of intelligence or potential.

In nurseries and schools we should celebrate the rich diversity of language and dialect and accent in our world. We need to develop a knowledge and understanding of the background culture from which these come. Only then will be able to help children to achieve their educational and intellectual potential.

✔ PROGRESS CHECK

1 Explain what a dialect is. Give two examples of dialect.
2 Why might children using a dialect be disadvantaged?
3 A child with a particular accent may be subject to stereotypical views. What might these be?

You need to know the meaning of the following words and phrases. Go back through the chapter to make sure you understand them:

balanced bilingual
bilingual
divergent thinking
ethnolinguistic groups
heritage language
institutional disregard
linguistic code
metalinguistic skills
monolingual
mother tongue
native speaker
stereotypes
tokenistic

FURTHER READING

The following books will help to increase your knowledge and understanding of bilingualism:

Baker, C. (1988) *Key Issues in Bilingualism and Bilingual Education, Multilingual Matters*, Cleveland Philadelphia
This book will help to develop better understanding of the value of bilingualism.

Baker, Colin and Prys Jones, Sylvia (1999) *Encyclopaedia of Bilingualism and Bilingual Education*, University of Wales
This book covers all aspects of world bilingualism. It is well worth looking for in a university library if you are researching bilingualism.

Romaine, S. (1994) *Bilingualism*, Blackwell
This book is an in-depth introduction to the study of bilingualism. It also assesses the positive and negative claims for the effects of bilingualism.

The child who is deaf

The key topics covered in this chapter are:

- Understanding deafness
- Manual communication
- Deaf bilingualism
- The education of children who are deaf.

The importance of children hearing spoken language around them is recognised by all developmental theorists. If a child is deaf or has impaired hearing the development of normal, oral language is affected. Almost all children who are deaf, or have impaired hearing, do learn oral language but the amount depends on many factors – their need to communicate orally, the community, deaf or hearing, where they spend most of their time, the type of education they have received and the severity or otherwise of their hearing disability.

Deaf communities in most countries have their own sign languages, which are languages in their own right. These are manual and visual ways of communicating. Many children who are deaf learn a sign language at home if it is used by the adults around them. Other children's first contact with a sign language will be when they enter a school where it is taught. For many children who are deaf sign language will be their first language and in the UK English and English in print will be their second and third languages. Deaf bilingualism should be valued as part of a diverse language structure and the right of every child who is deaf, whatever the level of his hearing loss, to grow up bilingual should be recognised.

A number of children will learn sign language when they enter school

UNDERSTANDING DEAFNESS

Incidence

Estimates of the numbers of children with hearing impairments vary. In the UK about 65,000 children have some form of hearing impairment. Only one in 1,000 of these children are born **profoundly deaf**, the other children having conditions that vary from mild to severe, with some children having conditions which vary in severity over time. One quarter of children will suffer from some form of hearing impairment before they are 7, usually due to an ear infection. The vast majority of these children will go on to have normal hearing.

Causes and types of hearing loss

There are two types of hearing loss:

- **conductive hearing loss**
- **sensori-neural hearing loss**.

Conductive hearing loss

This is where there is a problem in the transmission of sound from the outer ear to the middle ear. There are three main causes:

- *Infection* The most common cause of this form of deafness is infection of the middle ear (otitis media). Eighty per cent of children have had at least one attack before the age of 5. The middle ear becomes infected and produces pus which in extreme cases exerts so much pressure on the ear drum that it ruptures. The hearing loss is the result of loss of mobility of the middle ear mechanism. In some children the condition becomes chronic – the pus in the middle ear changes into a thick, glue-like substance. This will cause prolonged periods of hearing loss which fluctuate in severity.

- *Congenital abnormalities* Over half of the children with Down's syndrome have conductive deafness where there are often abnormalities of the ear and the children are particularly prone to middle-ear infections. Children with a cleft palate also have a high risk of hearing problems due to the deformity of the muscle of the palate which affects the Eustachian tube in the ear.

- *Blockages in the outer ear* Small children are prone to inserting objects, such as beads, into their ears. Once removed normal hearing is restored. A build-up of wax will cause deafness.

Sensori-neural hearing loss

This is hearing loss caused by damage to the sensory cells of the inner ear, or to the nervous system associated with hearing. There are three main causes.

- *Genetic factors* Over half of the children with this type of deafness are born into families with a history of deafness. Deafness may also be part of a cluster of symptoms associated with particular syndromes, such as Usher's syndrome, an inherited condition which causes moderate to severe hearing loss together with visual impairment.

- *Infections* If a mother contracts an infection in the first three months of pregnancy, there is a risk that the developing foetus may be damaged. Rubella (German measles) is one infection that is known to cause damage to the inner ear and babies born to mothers who contracted rubella during pregnancy have a high risk of sensori-neural hearing loss. After birth, a child's hearing may be affected by meningitis, measles, mumps and other viral infections.

- *Trauma* Lack of oxygen to the baby at birth may damage the nerve cells in the inner ear, as will severe jaundice in the new baby. Prematurity also increases the risk of deafness. After birth children may acquire sensori-neural deafness due to brain injury or as a rare side effect of the administration of some drugs.

The effects of hearing loss

Even a slight conductive hearing loss can affect a child's language development. Children who have a conductive hearing loss in the first six months of life have been shown to do less well on vocabulary tests and tests of auditory comprehension, when they are older. Educational achievement has been shown to be affected. Older children suffering from intermittent hearing loss due to repeated infections may fall behind in their school work and behavioural difficulties may develop.

Sensori-neural deafness varies from moderate to profound and is permanent. The effect depends on the nature of the impairment. An intelligent child with a moderate hearing loss and a supportive home may do very well, with only minimal effects. However, a child with the same hearing loss who is less advantaged in terms of intellect and home support may have considerable language difficulties, under-achieve at school and exhibit behavioural problems. Many children with a profound hearing loss will fail to develop oral language, but they may develop advanced language skills through lip reading and signing. With specialist teaching and support most children can achieve their educational potential.

THINK ABOUT IT

Think of a reason (or reasons) why a child who has conductive hearing loss in the first six months of life might do less well than what is considered age-appropriate in vocabulary tests or tests of auditory

Indications of children who may have a hearing impairment

It is essential that a child with a hearing impairment is identified as soon as possible. Any parental concerns should be taken seriously because they have intimate knowledge of their child. The following signs may indicate a cause for concern.

Birth–6 months

Signs of hearing impairment include a history provided by the parents that involves any of the causes already described and concerns that the baby:

- does not react in any way to loud noises
- does not awaken to loud noises
- does not freely imitate sound
- cannot be soothed by voice alone
- does not turn his head in the direction of his mother's voice.

6–12 months

Signs which give cause for concern include noticing that the child:

- does not point to familiar persons or objects when asked
- does not babble, or babbling has stopped
- by 12 months does not understand simple phrases such as 'wave bye bye', 'clap hands', without the aid of gestures.

13 months–2 years

Signs for concern include noticing that the child:

- does not accurately turn in the direction of a soft voice on the first call
- is not alert to environmental sounds
- does not respond to sound or does not locate where sound is coming from
- does not begin to imitate and use simple words for familiar people and things around the home
- does not sound, or use speech, like other children of the same age
- does not listen to TV at normal volume
- does not show consistent growth in the understanding and use of words to communicate.

The older child

In addition to the signs already noted, the older child may:

- show lack of attention
- look constantly at the speaker's face
- respond poorly to speech in noisy surroundings
- speak very loudly or quietly
- speak using a monotonous voice
- ask for questions to be repeated, or copies what older children are doing

- appear disruptive, show persistent temper tantrums and appear to day-dream
- show signs of lack of confidence and not wanting to go to school.

Types of hearing assessment

Behavioural tests

These are carried out on children old enough to respond to sounds either by turning their heads or by playing a game. These tests can be unreliable and can result in the child appearing to hear when in fact they are responding with their other senses to changes around them. Children can also appear to 'fail' the tests if they are tired, ill, inattentive or unco-operative. These tests include:

- the 'distraction test' – usually carried out on babies about 8 months old – sounds are made into the ears while the baby is distracted by a toy. The ability to hear is assessed by observing whether or not the baby turns to the sound

GOOD PRACTICE

- Always work in partnership with the child's parents/carers. Make sure they are aware of any concerns you may have.
- Liaise with any professionals involved in the care of the child so that there is consistency of approach.
- Implement the **1994 Code of Practice**.
- Become proficient in the method of communication that the child is using.
- Update your knowledge and understanding of the hearing impairment the child has.
- If a child is wearing hearing aids make sure you know how to fit and adjust them and can tell if they are working properly.
- Ensure you know how to change a battery in a hearing aid.
- Take time to ensure that the child knows the routine of the day and warn him in advance of any changes. Make sure that all staff and the child know what to do in the event of an emergency.
- Be aware that frustration can lead to behaviour difficulties. Try to ensure that the child does not become overtired.
- Be vigilant for any signs of bullying and implement the establishment's behaviour/anti-bullying policy if you suspect this to be the case.
- Have resources available that reflect positive images, for example, dolls with hearing aids, books and posters of children using signing.
- Before you talk to the child, make sure that you have his complete attention. Speak to the child by looking at him face-to-face, at his level.

- Speak normally, but more slowly. Do not shout at the child. Do not cover your mouth when you talk.
- When speaking to the child have the light in front of you, not behind you.
- Keep background noise to a minimum.
- As well as speech, use gestures and other forms of non-verbal communication. Always check that the child has understood what you want to communicate.

For older children

- Make the child welcome. Help him to find others with common interests and include him in extra-curricular activities.
- Encourage the child to take risks.
- Give lots of praise and encouragement.
- Arrange 'experiential learning' sessions, workshops, practical tasks, team work, etc.
- Give as much visual material as possible – handouts, board work, multi-media material and books.
- Investigate how technology can aid the child's performance, for instance, radio microphones and computers.
- Ensure that there are positive images of people with a hearing loss, not only in the resource material that you use, but also, if possible, in the adults who visit the classroom.
- Encourage other children to become proficient in the method of communication that the child is using.

- co-operative performance test – for older children: the ability to hear is assessed by observing whether or not a child obeys an instruction, for example 'Show me the duck', spoken into the ear
- pure tone audiometry – sounds are played into the child's ears via a headphone and the child has to indicate when a sound is heard.

Auditory brainstem evaluation

Sounds are presented to a child's ears through earphones while he sleeps. The responses in the brain are measured through small electrodes taped on his head and then analysed by computer. This assessment is carried out at birth.

Otoacoustic emissions

This measures the sounds that are 'sent out' by the nervous activity of the inner ear. A tiny microphone is placed in the ear canal of the baby and the sounds picked up are analysed by computer.

Neither the auditory brainstem evaluation or the otoacoustic emission need the child's active participation.

<table>
<tr><td>

DEFINITION

1994 Code of Practice a government document which sets out the principles and procedures for the identification, assessment and review of children with special educational needs in schools

</td></tr>
</table>

Make sure you know how to change a battery in a hearing aid

More information on developing the language and communication skills of a child who is deaf is given later in the chapter.

Treatments and interventions

Conductive hearing loss is usually treatable by use of antibiotics or surgery. Sensori-neural hearing loss is not treatable. However, there have been great advances in providing children with **cochlear implants**.

Hearing aids

There are several types of hearing aid for different conditions. They are designed to amplify all sound and do not produce normal hearing. Even profoundly deaf children may benefit from very high-powered aids. The earlier the child is fitted with a hearing aid the better the result will be. Children need adult support to wear hearing aids as they may attract teasing and bullying and the older child may be reluctant to wear one.

<table>
<tr><td>

DEFINITION

cochlear implant an implant which replaces the inner ear and electronically stimulates the nerve of hearing

</td></tr>
</table>

DEFINITIONS

sign language   the manual and gestural system of communication used by people who are deaf; the sign languages used in different countries are languages in their own right, and not manual means of communicating the spoken languages of those countries

Blissymbols   a universal language of pictographic symbols which is used by people with reading and writing disabilities

Makaton   a basic signing system using signs borrowed from British Sign Language, used by people who have severe learning difficulties

Braille   a touch-based reading and writing system used by people who are blind

British Sign Language (BSL) the sign language used by the deaf community in the UK

cued speech   a system of eight handshapes made in four locations near the face to assist children (or adults) who are deaf in lipreading

DO THIS!

If possible, watch television programmes where there is 'News for the Deaf' or a programme like 'See Hear' on the BBC. Note how finger spelling is used for names and unusual words.

✔ PROGRESS CHECK

1 What are the two main types of hearing impairment?
2 List three causes for one type of impairment.
3 What would lead you to suspect that a child of 2 had a hearing impairment?
4 In what ways would you support a 3-year-old child in a nursery class who had a moderate hearing loss and wore a hearing aid?

MANUAL COMMUNICATION

Manual communication refers to the various systems of communication which rely on the use of the hands and the whole body. It refers mainly to **sign languages** used by the deaf, but it also refers to the systems of communication using signs and/or symbols, for example, **Makaton**, **Blissymbols** and **Braille** which are used by people who may have difficulty using speech. Many people who are deaf use the sign language of the country they live in. In the UK the sign language used by the deaf community is known as **British Sign Language** (BSL). Children who are deaf also use sign language if they are given the opportunity to learn it. They may also learn (in the UK) Signed English in school, and **cued speech** (no longer used in UK schools) is used by a small percentage of children in America.

Signed languages

Signed languages make use of the hands mainly but also the body, head, face, eyes and mouth to communicate meanings. It is particularly important to realise that sign languages are not manual means of communicating English, or any other language. They are languages in their own right and they have their own structure and grammar and are capable of communicating abstract concepts in rich and varied ways. British, Irish and American people all speak English but their sign languages are all different. It is thought that sign languages go back to prehistoric times and they are mentioned in the Talmud (the Jewish holy book) and in the Bible. References to them appear in Greek and Roman writings. Sign languages are influenced by, and change like, other languages, when they come in contact with each other.

It is important to be aware that finger spelling, although it is an integral part of signing, since it is used for spelling names, novel words and specialised terms which have no manual sign, is generally regarded as a separate component of communication and is therefore not part of sign language itself.

The standard manual alphabet is used for spelling names, novel words and specialised terms in BSL

Signed English

Signed English mirrors spoken English. It has borrowed BSL signs with finger spelling and grammatical markers and it follows English word-order. Signed English was introduced into British schools in the 1980s as part of a drive to improve communication in schools for the deaf. Parents were taught it as well as children. Its advantages, particularly at the time it was introduced, were that:

- it enabled profoundly deaf children to communicate more quickly than if they had to rely on an **oral method** only. It can take a much longer time to become proficient at **lipreading**
- adults, both parents and teachers, found it easier to learn and use than BSL because it followed English word order
- it was helpful for children learning to read and useful for academic instruction.

There have been criticisms of the Signed English method as it was considered that:

- it was an arrogant approach. BSL is the natural language of the deaf but was not, at the time, valued as a suitable means of educating profoundly deaf children
- the bilingual approach was not valued. Children who are deaf will need to learn to use English in print and spoken English but it was not considered, at the time, that BSL was their first language, or that they were capable of learning a second or third language
- culture was not valued. By depriving children, even if only partially, of their heritage language they were also, to some extent, kept out of touch with **deaf culture**.

Cued speech

Cued speech is an oral language tool. It was used for about five years in some UK schools for the deaf. It is estimated that in America only 1 per cent of families with children who are deaf use it

It is a method of using hand signals to cue to the listener the English phonemes that are spoken. It is a **receptive system** invented by a hearing person. It consists of four vowel positions in the mouth and neck area and eight hand shapes to indicate consonants. It was/is used for academic instruction.

✔ PROGRESS CHECK

1 What is manual communication?
2 What is the difference between sign languages and other manual means of communicating a spoken language?
3 What is Signed English?
4 Why was Signed English introduced into UK schools in the 1980s?
5 Give one criticism of the Signed English method.

DEAF BILINGUALISM

It is only recently that we have begun to have an understanding of the language of people who are deaf. In 1988 the European Parliament passed a resolution on sign language proposing that every member state recognise its own national sign language as an official language of that country. This has not yet happened in the UK. The British Deaf Association have said that 'Deaf people have the same right to a quality education throughout their lives, which accepts their linguistic, cultural and social identity, which builds positive self-esteem and which sets no limits on their learning.'

It is still widely assumed that the first language of deaf people born in the UK is English. This is, and has been, deeply damaging to British deaf people educationally, culturally and politically. Until the 1980s BSL was not considered to be a language either by the deaf themselves or those in contact with them. Schools for children who were deaf considered deaf signing to be ungrammatical and a limited form of communication. At the end of the 1970s linguistic research in the United States on American Sign Language (ASL) and in the UK on BSL began to show that these sign languages *did* have a grammatical structure (which is different from English) and that it was indeed a full linguistic system.

At the present time in the UK some children who are deaf are still educated using the **auditory-oral method** but the majority are educated using spoken English and simultaneously signs borrowed from BSL. There is, however, increased recognition that BSL is the preferred or primary language of some deaf children. Where this is the case, these children are likely to benefit from an approach which sees English as their second language.

When considering deaf bilingualism the following points need to be kept in mind:

> ## DEFINITION
>
> **auditory-oral method**
> children are trained to use any hearing they have, to lip-read and to speak

- Any sign language is a language in its own right with its own grammatical rules and syntax.

- Sign language is not international. Sign languages evolved wherever there were groups of deaf people. British, Irish and American sign languages are all different. However, there are links between ASL and LSF (French Sign Language) because LSF was introduced into education for the deaf in the eighteenth century in America. There are also elements of spoken language which have been absorbed into the sign languages of the deaf.

- Sign language is not derived from the spoken language of the country to which it belongs.

- Sign languages have to be learned in the same way as any other language. This also applies to sign languages from English-speaking countries, ASL, BSL and ISL (Irish Sign Language), which shows their independence from English.

- The sign language used by people who are deaf cannot be fully considered as a heritage language or 'mother tongue' as deaf children do not always have deaf parents. It is nevertheless the first language of its users.

- Sign language and English in print constitute deaf bilingualism in English-speaking countries. Both languages are visually based and so are accessible to people who are deaf. Each language serves a specific function in everyday life and people who are deaf switch between both languages depending on need in the same way as hearing people switch between speaking and reading and writing.

- Many children and adults who are deaf learn to use spoken English, which may be considered a further additional language.
- The culture of people who are deaf is determined by living in an environment where experiences are predominantly visually-oriented. It is made up of the collective experience of people who are deaf.
- Just as any language helps its speakers to absorb the culture to which it belongs, so sign language help its users to absorb deaf culture.
- Children who are deaf benefit from having their language and culture valued.

✔ PROGRESS CHECK

1 What did research into sign language at the end of the 1970s in America show?

2 Can a person who uses British Sign Language automatically understand Irish Sign Language? Give reasons for your answer.

3 (a) What is the first language of many deaf people?

(b) What is usually their second language?

4 Explain what deaf bilingualism means.

THE EDUCATION OF CHILDREN WHO ARE DEAF

History of education for the deaf

For centuries children who were deaf, in any country, grew up in their families learning to cope as best they could and being part of whatever work the family was doing. They communicated using a mixture of signs, gesture, pantomime, speech and lipreading, but the term 'deaf and dumb' which was used until a few decades ago indicates that they were considered, for the most part, incapable of speech and quite often incapable of rational logical thinking too. Wherever groups of deaf people managed to get together, they developed their own sign languages, which were rich and complex, but not appreciated or understood in the hearing world.

Individuals from the hearing world who felt the need to come in contact with signing for religious or educational purposes surrounded this form of communication with secrecy. Catholic monks who learned a manual signing system often made a vow to keep it secret. Nevertheless, signing was sometimes spread by deaf boys who had been educated in monasteries and subsequently hired as teachers of deaf children by wealthy parents.

The world's first school for the deaf was at a mission at San Salvador near Madrid in the middle of the sixteenth century. It was destroyed by fire and

Abbé de l'Epée – the father of modern deaf education

all written records were lost. It was the Abbé Charles de l'Epée (1712–89), a French priest, who is now considered the father of modern education for the deaf. He founded the French National Institute in 1760, where deaf children were taught using sign language, with considerable success. Abbé de l'Epée broke with the secrecy of the past and established teacher training programmes.

The oralist tradition

The oralist movement which emphasised the importance of teaching speech as the first communication method had many supporters from the sixteenth to the nineteenth centuries. Sign language was often used in conjunction with speech and lipreading but the goal for oralists was a deaf population who could speak to all. Oralists believed in the moral superiority of spoken language and in their schools children who used signs to communicate were punished.

The most famous of the oralist schools was that of Thomas Braidwood (1715–1806), a mathematics teacher, who established the first school for the deaf in Edinburgh in 1767 based on the oral method. Braidwood was secretive about his method but the school did use some signing. However, the end result was speech and it is believed that Braidwood was one of those who believed in the moral superiority of spoken language. It seems that the gift of speech was confused with the gift of reason.

Throughout the nineteenth century, schools for the deaf continued to be opened both in Europe and in the USA. The controversy of oralism versus signing continued. In 1880 in Milan there was a world-wide conference on the education of deaf children. After much discussion the conference adopted a recommendation to recognise oralism as the preferred mode of communication. This was accepted by all delegates except those from the USA and that acceptance is now seen as a 'dark day' for deaf culture.

The twentieth century

It was only in the twentieth century with the development of modern linguistics that it was finally recognised that sign languages are as complex in structure as any oral language and can express abstract concepts just as well. The controversy between oralism and signing still continues but in the late 1970s it was recognised that communication – using any method – was really important for the educational development of children. British schools introduced a method known as 'total communication', which uses a combination of Signed English, speech and lipreading.

In the 1980s and 1990s there was a growing awareness of both the value of bilingualism as a positive force in any adult's or child's life and the recognition of the fact that deaf children could develop very successfully as bilinguals. By knowing and using both a sign language and an oral language (in its written and, where possible, its spoken form) the child will attain his full cognitive, linguistic and social capabilities.

KEY TERMS

You need to know the meaning of the following words and phrases. Go back through the chapter to make sure you understand them:

auditory-oral method
Blissymbols
Braille
British Sign Language (BSL)
cochlear implant
conductive hearing loss
cued speech
deaf culture
lipreading
Makaton
oral method
profoundly deaf
receptive system
sensori-neural hearing loss
sign language

✔ PROGRESS CHECK

1 How were deaf children taught in the Abbé de l'Epée's school in France in the eighteenth century?
2 What did oralists in past centuries believe about spoken language?
3 What recommendation was adopted by the Milan conference in 1880 about deaf education?
4 How is this recommendation viewed at the present time?
5 Explain 'total communication'.

FURTHER READING

Ree, Jonathan (1999) *I See a Voice*, Harper Collins
   This is a study of the philosophical history of language, deafness and the senses. It would be helpful for getting a more in-depth understanding of the history of deaf education for an undergraduate course.
Dare, A. and O'Donovan, M. (1997) *Good Practice in Working with Children with Special Needs*, Stanley Thornes
   This is a key text for all Early Years workers and students. It provides valuable information on the care and education of children with disabilities, as well as setting out the current legislation and the statutory provision affecting them.

Language and communication problems

PREVIEW

The key topics covered in this chapter are:

- Stammering (stuttering)
- Developmental verbal dyspraxia
- Autism
- Dyslexia.

For most children the development of spoken and written language occurs relatively smoothly. However, for some children, the process of acquiring language and literacy is more difficult and they will require professional help. In the UK it has been suggested that one child in 1,000 needs specialist help in acquiring language, although perhaps as many as 10 per cent of children have mild difficulties that do not need specialist treatment.

This chapter describes some of the more common conditions and provides information to help you identify possible difficulties and guidelines for caring for children with these conditions.

DEFINITION

stammering an abnormal speech pattern where there are hesitations and repetitions that break the flow of speech

STAMMERING (STUTTERING)

Stammering is a condition where there are breaks in the flow of speech. According to the British Stammering Association stammering speech is characterised by a child:

- putting extra effort into saying words
- having tense and jerky speech
- seeming not to get started – no sound comes out for several seconds

- stretching sounds in words (*I want a ssstory*)
- repeating parts of words several times (*mu-mu-mummy*)
- stopping what they are saying halfway through a sentence.

Incidence

It is estimated that between 5 and 15 per cent of children stammer at some point in their childhood. Although many children overcome the difficulty, about 1 per cent of the population as a whole stammer. The typical age for stammering to begin is between 2 and 3 years old. There are equal numbers of boys and girls who stammer at this age, but as children grow older more boys than girls are affected, so that by adulthood 80 per cent of stammerers are men.

Identification of children who may have a problem

It is normal for children to stumble over their words when they are learning to talk. Many children will not be fluent when they are under pressure to communicate competently. It is normal for young children sometimes to repeat whole words at the beginning of a phrase or when thinking of how to finish a sentence. Children may also use *ums* and *ers* when they are sorting out what to say next. An excited or nervous child will be more prone to this type of error. However, a child who often gets stuck on words, repeating or prolonging parts of words or who puts excessive effort into speaking, may be at risk of developing a stammer.

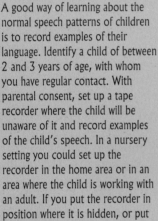

DO THIS!

A good way of learning about the normal speech patterns of children is to record examples of their language. Identify a child of between 2 and 3 years of age, with whom you have regular contact. With parental consent, set up a tape recorder where the child will be unaware of it and record examples of the child's speech. In a nursery setting you could set up the recorder in the home area or in an area where the child is working with an adult. If you put the recorder in position where it is hidden, or put the recorder in the same place frequently, you will have more chance of the child acting naturally.

When you have recorded the child speaking you will be able to play it back and write down exactly what the child has said. Using the information from the previous section, identify the dysfluencies (see below) in the child's speech. The more recordings you make of children of various ages, the greater will be your understanding of normal speech patterns in children.

Set up the tape recorder in the home area

Identifying children who need professional help (pre-school)
The British Stammering Association has produced a set of guidelines for child-care practitioners to use when deciding whether or not to refer a child for speech and language therapy. They are as follows.

DEFINITION

dysfluent speech speech that is not smooth and continuous, often heard in young children

The child has **dysfluent speech** and one or more of the following factors are present:

- a family history of stammering or speech or language problems
- the child is finding learning to talk difficult in any way
- the child shows signs of frustration or is upset by his speaking
- the child is struggling when talking
- the child is in a dual language situation and is stammering in her first language
- there is parental concern or uneasiness
- the child's general behaviour is causing concern.

Phases in the development of stammering

If early identification and referral to a speech and language therapist is not made in the pre-school years, untreated stammering may get progressively worse. In primary school the child's stammering is likely to become chronic and not just set off by pressure or excitement. The child sees herself as a stammerer. The child's stammering behaviour will vary according to the situation she is in. Syllables and words that cause trouble are identifiable. The child starts to avoid words and becomes irritated with the problem. By secondary school she may begin to avoid speaking situations. She will anticipate problems and approach speaking situations with fear. In late adolescence and adulthood the stammerer starts to feel embarrassed about the problem.

THINK ABOUT IT

Consider the nature v. nurture debate (see page 30) and think of ways in which stammering could be caused either by factors affecting the child before birth or factors that have caused the child to stammer after birth.

Theories about stammering

There are four main types of theory about why a child may develop a stammer:

- *Organic theories* These theories are based on the findings that there are differences in the brains of stammerers and non-stammerers. These differences may result in dysfluent speech. On the other hand, some people hold the opinion that dysfluent speech causes the changes in the brain.
- *Genetic theories* A child who stammers is three times more likely to have a relative who stammers than a child who does not stammer. This suggests that there may be a genetic component to stammering.
- *Psychoanalytic theory* This suggests that stammering is a symptom of hostility and recommends psychotherapy as treatment. This is not a theory that has much support today.
- *Learning theory* All children go through a stage when they appear to stammer, particularly if they are excited or nervous. If they are corrected by adults who tell them to 'slow down' or 'take a deep breath', the children's attention is drawn to their speech and they start to struggle to overcome dysfluencies. The children may become anxious and this increased anxiety may then result in increased stammering.

None of these theories are proven – stammering is very likely to be due to a combination of factors that interact in a complex way.

GOOD PRACTICE

These guidelines are based on those suggested by the British Stammering Association.

For young children

- Speak slowly to all children. It will help the child who is dysfluent without drawing attention to her by asking her to slow down.
- Try to speak to the child at her level, both physically and by using language that she can understand.
- Reduce the number of questions you ask the child.
- Try to give alternatives so that the child can answer with a short response.
- Comment on the emotions or the events that are causing the child to be dysfluent rather than the specific words, for instance 'I can see that you are very cross'.
- Some situations help children become more fluent, such as speaking together with other children, reciting rhymes that have a strong rhythm, singing and counting together. This will help children without drawing attention to them.
- Some situations will cause a child's stammering to increase, for instance being interrupted or hurried, fear of the consequences of what's being said, expressing complex ideas and using new vocabulary.
- It is recommended that you observe the child and keep a record of what increases and decreases the stammering.
- Many children who stammer have periods when their language is fluent. When this happens the carer should take the opportunity to develop oral skills.
- Some children may need extra help when learning to read, since uncertainty about a particular word may precipitate stammering. Giving a child something concrete to do when faced with a new word may help, for instance sounding out the word.
- Children are more fluent when they are talking about a subject that really interests them. They are also helped by using visual aids, for example to demonstrate something they have made, whilst they are speaking.
- Try not to become anxious yourself as this will communicate itself to the child and increase difficulties.
- Listen carefully to the child so that there is no need to repeat what is said.

Older children

Older children who stammer are probably receiving some sort of speech and language therapy. It is essential that you liaise with parents and therapist so that there is consistency in approach. As a child grows older the emotional and social effects of stammering become more apparent. It is vital that the child is not put into situations where her stuttering will lead her to lose self-esteem. As with all children, recognition of success in other areas will raise self-esteem and direct attention away from the stammering. It is important that older children feel relaxed and do not feel they have to cover up their stammering. If this degree of trust can be reached in the classroom, they will be able to speak more fluently.

Teasing/bullying

Children who are 'different' are at risk of being teased or bullied. Because the older child often feels ashamed of her stammering she may find teasing particularly hard to cope with. Any teasing or bullying within the classroom should be taken very seriously and the establishment's anti-bullying policy should be put into effect. The class should be led into discussions about teasing and bullying in general. All children should be left in no doubt about what is considered unacceptable behaviour, without drawing attention to the child who is being teased. Children with few friends are more at risk of bullying and the child-care practitioner should endeavour to help the child who stammers integrate well with the other children and make friends.

Treatments and interventions

There are many different approaches to helping children who stammer. Modern approaches are very effective in reducing dysfluency in a child's speech. However, for treatment to be most successful the child needs to be referred to a speech and language therapist as soon as possible. The speech and language therapist will work closely with the parents/carers of the child. A full history of the child's development will be taken and the therapist will make an assessment of the child's language needs. Any treatment programme will involve the parents working in partnership with the therapist.

For pre-school children therapy could involve a series of sessions with the therapist working with the parent and the child, followed up by several review sessions to see if progress is maintained. With older children the therapy could include graded activities designed to modify speech, social skills training, problem-solving, and other activities designed to increase self-esteem and confidence. Therapy will involve individual sessions, family interaction sessions, group therapy and role play.

Electronic aids

There are several electronic aids that can help people who stammer. These devices are usually used in conjunction with speech therapy and are for older individuals with severe problems.

Alternative treatments

Alternative treatments include acupuncture, hypnosis and relaxation/stress reduction techniques. These techniques are not proven to be very successful in reducing stammering, but may help in general relaxation and stress reduction.

✔ PROGRESS CHECK

1 What is stammering?
2 What signs would indicate that a pre-school aged child might be at risk of developing a stammer?
3 How could you meet the needs of a 4-year-old child in the nursery who was having speech therapy for a stammer, if you were the child's key worker?
4 How might the needs of a 7-year-old child with a stammer differ from those of a 4-year-old child?

DEVELOPMENTAL VERBAL DYSPRAXIA (DVD)

This is also known as developmental apraxia. The term 'dyspraxia' can be confusing because it means different things to different people. If you were talking to physiotherapists they would use the term to describe children who have difficulty co-ordinating their gross and fine motor skills and who may be described as being 'clumsy'. In this book we are using the term to describe a speech and language difficulty. **Developmental verbal dyspraxia** is said to occur when a child has difficulties in producing speech sounds and putting these sounds together in the correct sequence to form words. Often expressive language (spoken language) is delayed. Frequently children will also have an oro-motor dyspraxia which means that they cannot co-ordinate the movement of the mouth, lips, tongue and palate to make correct speech sounds.

The condition has been compared to watching a cable TV station without the right descrambler. There is nothing wrong with the TV station and there is nothing wrong with the TV set. It's just that the set cannot read the signal that the station is sending out. In other words, the condition is not a muscle disorder, nor is it a cognitive disorder. The child's language learning task is to somehow unscramble the mixed messages her brain is sending to her muscles.

> ### DEFINITION
>
> **developmental verbal dyspraxia** a condition where a child has difficulties in producing speech sounds and in putting these sounds together in the correct sequence to form words

163

The condition may occur on its own or the child may have additional conditions, for instance, autism (see page 168), cerebral palsy or Down's syndrome.

Identification of children who may have a problem

You may observe some of the following features:

- The child's abilities to understand language (receptive language ability) is broadly within normal limits, but her expressive speech is seriously deficient, absent or severely unclear.

- The child has a quiet voice.

- There is poor lip control, an open mouthed posture and dribbling.

- The child may make involuntary movements of the mouth and tongue when trying to speak.

- The child can only use a few consonants, such as *h* and *d*, but has a better range of vowels.

- The child shows difficulty in sequencing sounds.

- The parents may report a history of language difficulties in the family.

- The child may have been born premature, have had a difficult delivery or have a history of illness affecting the brain.

Associated features of developmental verbal dyspraxia

The child may go on to experience difficulties in reading, spelling or maths. Some children have fine motor difficulties making certain tasks such as handwriting, more difficult, but others do not have these problems.

Causes of developmental verbal dyspraxia

The condition is generally regarded as being caused by an abnormality in the brain. The abnormality may be present before birth, be caused by a difficult birth, accident or illness after birth.

Conditions associated with DVD occurring before or at birth include:

- pre-maturity
- placental problems
- umbilical cord around the neck at delivery
- **meconium** passed before birth
- failure of the new-born baby to suck properly.

THINK ABOUT IT

1 What might be the connection between the first four conditions listed below and DVD?
2 What may be the connection between failure to suck and DVD?

DEFINITION

meconium the first stool a baby passes after birth. If passed before birth it may indicate that the baby is in distress

GOOD PRACTICE

- Early diagnosis and treatment is essential, with the best results being with children who start therapy at about 3 years of age.
- You need to act on any concerns you may have about a child as soon as possible.
- There should be an active partnership between the child-care practitioner, the parents and the speech and language therapist so that any treatment can be reinforced in the nursery/school.
- The establishment's special needs policy needs to be implemented and the child assessed under the 1994 Code of Practice for children with special educational needs.
- The child will benefit from lots of one-to-one therapy with frequent repetitions of sounds, sound sequences and movement patterns in order to incorporate them and make them automatic.
- Mealtimes can be adapted to encourage the development of lip and mouth muscles, for instance include items in the diet that require chewing, such as apples, celery and carrots. Ice cream or chocolate can be smeared on the child's lips and the child encouraged to lick them off. This encourages the development of the tongue and lip muscles. Blowing bubbles will also encourage the co-ordination of mouth muscles.
- Some children will be taught a signing system such as Makaton (see below). If this is the case, you will need to be familiar with the signs so that they can support the child.
- Encourage the child to use vocal language in everyday situations, without putting her under undue pressure.
- It is important that you are relaxed, and praise the child when she succeeds in other areas so that her self-esteem is raised. Be aware that the child may attract teasing or bullying and deal with the situation as discussed previously.

Blowing bubbles will encourage the co-ordination of mouth muscles

DO THIS!

Collect all the policies in your establishment that may be relevant to the care of a child with DVD. You should be able to obtain the policy for special educational needs and the anti-bullying/behaviour policy. If you are part of a group, compare policies from a variety of establishments. You may find that some policies need revising.

Makaton

Makaton is a signing system devised by a speech therapist in the 1970s to help adults with severe learning difficulties to communicate. It is a basic means of communication and it encourages language development in children and adults with communication difficulties. Makaton signs are borrowed from British Sign Language, or from the sign language of the country in which it is used. The signs are selected to communicate basic concepts which are graded in complexity. Basic information is given in a very visual way and spoken word order is used, with signs accompanying normal grammatical speech. Even with individuals who have limited language ability and poor retention, a basic vocabulary of Makaton signs will be very useful.

boy
Brush right index pointing left across chin

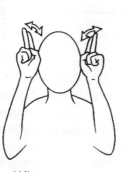

rabbit
Palm forward 'N' hands, held at either side of head, bend several times to indicate ears

fish
Right flat hand waggles forward like a fish swimming

bird
Index finger and thumb open and close in front of mouth like a beak

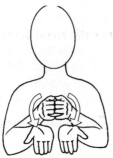

book
Two flat hands pointing forward, palm to palm, open to palms up

tree
Right elbow cradled in left hand. Right clawed hand, palm up/left twists from side to side

cup
Left hand, palm up. Rest blade of right wholehanded 'C' on left palm

baby
Mime cradling a baby in the arms and rock

give
Stroke right side of mouth with side of extended right index, palm forward

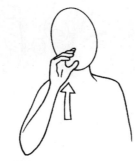

drink
Mime having a drink

cat
Open hands at sides of mouth move out slightly twice whilst flexing to indicate whiskers

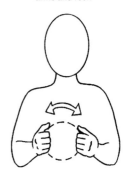

car
Mime holding and moving a steering wheel

coat
Mime pulling a coat over shoulders

bicycle
Two fists held a few inches apart make pedalling action

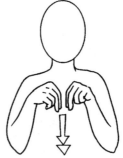

dog
Two 'N' hands pointing down, move up and down slightly, like dog begging

biscuit
Fingertips of right clawed hand tap near left elbow twice

Some Makaton signs

166

Treatments and interventions

There are various techniques available and although they differ from each other they do have common features. These include:

- principles of motor learning such as repetition and drill, correction and feedback and speaking at a slowed rate
- use of rhythm and melody
- using all the senses to help control sequences of movement, such as vision, touch and hearing.

Most therapists use a variety of methods based on an assessment of the child's individual needs.

CASE STUDY

Jack

Jack is aged 3½. He has just entered nursery class and it is immediately apparent that his speech is very unclear; only his mother and older sibling can understand him. On observation his key worker finds out that he understands what is said to him, that he is rather soft spoken, can use about three consonants and most of the vowel sounds. He finds it difficult sequencing sounds and appears to find it hard to co-ordinate his lips and tongue. His mother tells the key worker that he has been having regular speech therapy since he was 3 and has shown some improvement. It has been observed that Jack is finding it difficult to socialise with the other children. On at least one occasion a child has been heard to say 'Go away! You talk funny'.

1 What other information does the key worker need to have from the mother?
2 How could the key worker help Jack integrate with the other children?
3 How might the negative attitudes of the other children be handled?
4 When planning for Jack's care in the nursery, what should be the main aims of the nursery team?

✔ PROGRESS CHECK

1 Describe the main features of developmental verbal dyspraxia.
2 What other terms are used for this condition?
3 What areas of development may be affected in children with this condition, other than speech?
4 What may be the causes of this condition?
5 As a child-care practitioner, how would you help a child in your care who has this condition?

DEFINITIONS

autism   a disability that prevents individuals understanding the world around them through their senses, with associated problems in communication, social relationships and behaviour

Asperger syndrome   a condition similar to autism where an individual has difficulty communicating and relating to others, but who has appropriate language skills and does not have learning difficulties

metaphor   a figure of speech where something is described by stating another thing. For instance, **his words stabbed at her heart**

AUTISM

Autism is a lifelong developmental disability that prevents individuals from properly understanding the world around them through their senses. This results in severe problems of social relationships, communication and behaviour. Children with autism can vary in the severity of their symptoms, but all those who are affected will have difficulties in three areas – imagination, verbal and non-verbal communication, and social relationships.

There is a mild form of autism called **Asperger syndrome**. People with this condition also show difficulties in communicating and relating to others, but they have fewer problems with language than those with autism. People with Asperger syndrome do not have learning difficulties and are often of average or above average intelligence.

Incidence

Estimates of the prevalence of autism in the UK vary from 0.2 to 0.02 per cent, according to the definition used. Autism is distributed throughout the world, among all races, nationalities and social classes. Four out of every five children with autism are male. In addition, 75 per cent of children with autism have a learning disability, although occasionally a child with autism may be of above average intelligence.

Identification of children who may have a problem

The identification features of autism fall into four groups:

- difficulty with verbal and non-verbal communication
- difficulty with social relationships
- difficulty with developing imagination
- associated characteristics.

Difficulty with verbal and non-verbal communication

- There may be severe delays in language development. The child may be silent when playing.
- If the child has developed language, her language may include peculiar speech patterns or the use of words without attachment to their normal meanings, for instance, she may constantly repeat single words and phrases. If you ask the child a question, she may repeat it back to you, without answering
- The child may avoid eye contact when being spoken to.
- An older child may have developed speech but will tend to use unusual **metaphors** and may speak in a formal, monotonous way.
- The child may be able to ask for her own needs but will find it difficult to talk about feelings and thoughts and will not understand emotions.
- The child may not understand the meaning of gestures, facial expressions and tone of voice.

Difficulty with social relationships

- The child may show severe delays in understanding social relationships.

- The child may resist being picked up and cuddled.

- The child may appear to take no notice of the other children around her and may not play co-operatively with them.

- The older child may show an inability to develop friendships and an impaired ability to understand other people's feelings.

- If the child makes an approach to another child, it will often be in an odd, inappropriate, repetitive way, paying little attention to responses of those she approaches.

Difficulty with developing imagination

- The child may be unable to play imaginatively with objects or toys around her. She may focus on minor or trivial things, for example an earring rather than the person wearing it, or a wheel instead of the whole toy train.

- The child will be unable to engage in role-play.

- The child may perform repetitive body movements such as hand flicking, twisting, spinning, or rocking.

- The child may spend her time in repetitive activities, such as arranging and organising objects such as bottle tops, leaves and containers.

- The older child may become fascinated with memorising facts or making collections of objects with no regard to its importance or lack of it.

Associated characteristics

- The child may become dominated by routines and rituals. She may show great distress if the schedule is changed. For example, whilst dressing the child's clothes may always have to be put on in the same sequence, the same route may have to be taken to school every day.

- The child may show inconsistent responses to sensory input. For example, she may appear to be deaf and fail to respond to words and other sounds, but at other times she will be extremely distressed by an every-day noise such as a vacuum cleaner or a dog barking. The child may show an apparent insensitivity to pain and a lack of responsiveness to cold or heat, or may over-react to any of these.

Causes of autism

Autism is a disorder of the brain which affects the way the brain uses information. The exact causes have not yet been fully established. Some research suggests there is a physical problem affecting those parts of the brain that process language and information coming in from the senses. There may be an imbalance of certain chemicals in the brain. There is evidence that autism can be caused by a variety of conditions affecting brain development and which can occur before, during or after birth. Conditions which have been implicated include: maternal rubella, lack of oxygen at birth and complications of childhood illnesses, such as whooping cough and measles. Genetic factors may sometimes be involved. It is likely that a combination of factors are involved.

GOOD PRACTICE

- Liaise closely with the parents of the child. If the child has been diagnosed, work co-operatively with the parents and the professionals so that any treatment programme can be reinforced.
- Implement the establishment's special educational needs policy and the 1994 Code of Practice.
- Give as much one-to-one attention as resources will allow.
- Remember that the child may take everything you say literally. Your speech should be clear, spoken directly to the child, using simple vocabulary with no metaphors or exaggerations.
- Check that the child is listening to you, check that the child has understood what you have said.
- Involve the child in music activities, songs and rhymes.
- Help the child develop listening skills by encouraging her to clap a rhythm. Group music activities are particularly helpful.
- Activities designed to develop social skills are an important part of management. Activities requiring the child to co-operate with one other child should be tried first before expecting her to interact with a large group of children. Activities could include playing on the seesaw, taking turns to push another child on a truck, taking turns to brush each other's hair. When you discover an activity that the child enjoys, repeat it as a reward.
- Be aware that the child may be teased by the other children because she is different. Other children will find an autistic child very difficult to relate to. Act immediately, if the child is being bullied.
- A child with autism may have little idea of safety. For instance, there is a danger that the child will not realise when something is hot and will also be at risk of wandering off when outside.
- Autistic children are likely to have fixed routines involving all aspects of care, for instance, mealtimes, bedtimes, toileting and dressing. Sometimes these routines can be inconvenient and time wasting. However, it will not be possible to alter these routines all at once. Any attempt will need to be planned so that it involves a series of very small changes, with children being rewarded for appropriate behaviour. Behavioural management needs to involve the whole child-care team, the parents and appropriate professionals such as the educational psychologist.

Group music activities are particularly helpful for a child with autism

Carl

Carl is 3 and lives with his mother and baby brother (aged 3 months). Carl has been diagnosed as being autistic and started attending nursery one month ago. He has a full-time place, not only for his developmental needs, but also to give his mother a break during the day. Recently his father has left the family because the strain of caring for Carl and the new baby have proved too much. The family live on the fifth floor of a high-rise block in a run-down inner-city area. The mother does not work because of her child-care commitments and the family rely on state benefits to survive.

Carl has proved to be a difficult child to handle. His ritualistic behaviour has reached the extent that his mother is always late bringing him to nursery because it takes so long to get him ready in the mornings. If he sees a dog on the way to nursery he becomes very frightened and refuses to move. He is a large child and is getting heavy. In the nursery his key worker has not been able to form a relationship with him. He does not socialise and spends long periods of time sorting the bricks into colours. He becomes aggressive if other children disturb him or want to play with the bricks.

1 What are the likely difficulties facing Carl's mother?
2 What should be his key worker's priorities when planning for his care?
3 What **statutory** and/or **voluntary provision** is there to support Carl and his family?
4 List the professionals that may be involved in Carl's care.

DEFINITIONS

statutory provision
provision (services) which has to be provided by law

voluntary provision
provision (services) that meets a need within the community but which does not have to be provided by law

Treatments and interventions

As yet there is no cure for autism, but there are treatment programmes that result in considerable improvement in the child. Through specially trained teachers and the use of structured programmes that emphasise individual instruction, children with autism have been able to mature into adults who can function at home and in the community. Some can lead nearly normal lives, although some individuals will never be able to live independently.

✔ PROGRESS CHECK

1 What areas of development are most likely to be affected in a child with autism?
2 Which sex is most affected?
3 What is thought to be the cause of autism?
4 Is autism treatable?
5 List two things that will encourage speech development in a child with autism.
6 List two things that will encourage social development in a child with autism.

DYSLEXIA

Dyslexia is a condition where children of normal intelligence have unexpected difficulty in learning to read and write. Although the condition is primarily a difficulty with reading and spelling, there are often difficulties seen in visual/auditory perception, motor skills, rhyming skills, spoken language, short-term memory, planning, sequencing and telling left from right.

Children with dyslexia will experience difficulties throughout their lives, but most will learn strategies that help them cope most of the time. Many, with appropriate help, will be able to go onto further and higher education. Many children with dyslexia grow into adults who are valued because of their creative thinking and problem-solving abilities.

Incidence

Estimates vary, but the most commonly reported figure is that 4 per cent of the population are severely affected, with up to 10 per cent showing some signs of dyslexia. It used to be thought that boys were four times as likely to have dyslexia than girls, but recent research indicates that the condition may be more evenly spread across the genders. The incidence of dyslexia is unaffected by race, socio-economic status or level of intelligence.

Identification of children who may have a problem

According to the British Dyslexia Association there are a variety of signs that indicate that a child may have dyslexia, although some children do not show all the signs and some children have characteristics not mentioned on the list. *In particular, most pre-school children will show one or two of these signs and this does not mean that they are dyslexic.*

Pre-school signs which may indicate dyslexia
These include:

- a family history of dyslexia
- later than expected learning to speak clearly
- jumbled phrases, such as *teddy dare* for *teddy bear*
- quick thinker and do-er
- use of substitute words or 'near misses'
- mis-labelling, for instance, *lamp shade* for *lamp post*
- a lisp – *duckth* for *ducks*
- inability to remember the label for known objects, such as colours
- confused directional words, for instance, *up/down* or *in/out*
- excessive tripping, bumping and falling over nothing
- enhanced creativity – often good at drawing with a good sense of colour
- obvious 'good' and 'bad' days for no apparent reason
- aptitude for constructional or educational toys including computer keyboards

- enjoys being read to, but shows no interest in letters or words
- difficulty in learning nursery rhymes
- finds difficulty with rhyming words, such as *cat mat fat*
- finds difficulty with odd-one-out, for instance, *cat mat pig fat*
- did not crawl – was a bottom shuffler
- difficulty with sequence, for instance copying a coloured bead sequence
- appears 'bright' – seems an enigma.

For children of 9 or under

Signs include:

- particular difficulty in learning to read and write
- persistent and continued reversing of numbers and letters, such as 15 for 51 or *b* for *d*
- difficulty in telling left from right
- difficulty in learning the alphabet and multiplication tables, and remembering sequences such as the days of the week and the months of the year
- continued difficulty with shoelaces, ball catching and skipping
- inattention and poor concentration
- frustration, possibly leading to behavioural problems.

Causes of dyslexia

There are many theories about the causes of dyslexia. Some studies have demonstrated the presence of slight abnormalities in the brain. The possibility that dyslexia may be the result of an abnormality in the brain is strengthened by the fact that premature babies and babies who have had a difficult time immediately after birth have an increased risk of dyslexia. Whatever the cause, the processing and transmitting of sensory information (from the ears and the eyes) has been affected. The findings that some children with dyslexia come from families where several individuals have similar difficulties indicate that inheritance may be a factor.

GOOD PRACTICE

Partnership with parents

As with all children with special needs, it is essential that there is a positive partnership between the child's parents and the child-care practitioners. If you have concerns about a child, you need to inform the parents. Parents have expert knowledge of their child and will have much to offer to assessments. You can support parent's efforts to help their children by devising an appropriate programme for the child where activities carried out in nursery are reinforced at home.

Pre-school children

Because it is difficult, and perhaps unwise, to diagnose a child as having dyslexia in the pre-school years, these recommendations are designed to be of benefit to all children.

- Take time to listen carefully to the child and to answer her questions. Always check that the child understands what you have said and get her to repeat instructions back to you.
- Read to the child on a regular basis. You need to be particularly skilful so that you keep the child's attention. The use of story props together with rhymes, that the child can join in with, are particularly helpful.
- When you are reading a book show the child that, in English, the

words go from left to right and from top to bottom. The child may need to be taught how to hold a book and the direction in which to turn the pages.

- Include music and drama activities that contain lots of rhyming and repetition. Use actions to back up songs and rhymes.
- Children with dyslexia often find it difficult to dress themselves due to poor co-ordination, difficulty in sequencing and problems in identifying left and right. They will need constant practice in putting on their clothes and activities that encourage these skills are valuable. There should be a wide selection of dressing-up clothes, dolls and props that encourage the doing up of buttons and the tying of laces. The children's shoes may need to be marked so that they recognise left from right.
- Motor co-ordination may be affected so activities such as throwing and catching a large ball, balancing and using the outside play equipment are helpful. Fine co-ordination can be encouraged by painting with short stubby brushes and finger painting.
- Other activities that are of benefit include: laying the table (emphasising left and right), activities such as cooking, picture lotto, sorting tasks and board games that involve counting and taking turns.
- You will need to recognise any signs of stress since tasks that seem effortless to most children will require extra effort and determination for a child with dyslexia. Build times of quiet play into the day so that the child can build up her energy reserves again.
- Above all it is essential that the child is not made to feel a failure. There will be activities that the child is particularly good at and her success must be emphasised.

The primary school child

As with the pre-school child, good practice for a child with dyslexia will benefit all children. The British Dyslexia Association have the following suggestions.

- The child with dyslexia should sit near to the teacher so that the teacher can observe, help and encourage her to ask for help when required.
- However carefully the child is taught anything connected with written language, for instance the silent **e** rule, it must not be assumed that the child will remember and be able to use it. Constant over-learning is essential at every stage.
- Avoid indicating that the child is slow, lazy or stupid or comparing her written work with the other members of the class.
- The child should not be asked to read aloud in front of the class unless she particularly wants too.
- The child's ability should be judged more on her oral response than her written response.
- The child should not be expected to use a dictionary to find out

how to spell a word. Efficient dictionary skills need to be taught.

- The child should not be given long lists of mixed words to be learned every week. Give a few words of a family of words, such as **flight, light, sight**, etc.
- Copying out corrections several times may be of little help. Instead the following strategy should be used. The child-care practitioner copies out the word correctly. The child should look at it carefully, noting any tricky parts, and write several times over the top of the original, naming the letters as she does so. The child should then cover the word and try and write it from memory. The child then checks the word. If the child is correct she ticks it, otherwise the procedure is repeated. Be aware that the child may not be able to spell the word correctly at a later stage when writing an essay and her mind is engaged in other ideas.
- Wherever possible the child should be encouraged to repeat back what he has been asked to do – this also includes messages.
- The design and presentation of worksheets needs to be carefully thought out, with bold headings, clear print, less writing, more diagrams.

Practical ideas

- Wherever appropriate, use individual tuition or small groups.
- Try to discover how the child learns best and adapt your methods to suit her learning style.
- Use teaching programmes specifically designed for dyslexic pupils.
- Plan work so that it is at the correct level for the individual child.
- Work should have the occasional elements of discovery and open-endedness to motivate and interest the dyslexic pupil's creative mind.
- Rewards should be frequent, but only when deserved.
- Working environment should be quiet, non-distracting and attractive.
- Copying from the board is often a problem. Think of alternative methods. Seat the child near to and facing the board and use different coloured chalks or pens.
- Content rather than presentation should be the focus.
- Mark the child's work with the child sitting next to you. Do not correct too many errors at the same time. Set manageable targets.
- Encourage the use of word-processors, computers, calculators and tape recorders.
- Understand the intermittent nature of the child's performance and attention.
- All efforts should be made to build the child's confidence through identification and development of activities they do well.
- Show patience, understanding, encouragement and friendship, particularly when working with children who you think may be dyslexic.

DEFINITION

over-learning   the use of constant repetition and practice of a skill such as letter formation

Motor co-ordination may be affected by dyslexia, so activities such as throwing and catching a large ball are helpful

Treatments and interventions

If there are suspicions that a child is dyslexic, she will need an assessment which ideally will involve an educational psychologist, a speech and language therapist and an optometrist. Once a comprehensive assessment has been made then an appropriate programme can be designed for the child. There are three main approaches:

- developmental
- corrective
- remedial.

Developmental
This is sometimes described as the 'more of the same' approach. In this approach, teachers uses the same methods that have been tried previously but give the child extra attention and individual tuition. This method is not effective for many children.

Corrective
The corrective reading approach uses small groups in tutorial sessions, but it emphasises the child's assets and interests. Those who use this method hope to encourage children to rely on their own special abilities to overcome their difficulties.

Remedial
In this approach the instructor recognises the child's abilities but directs teaching mainly at the child's deficiencies. With careful assessment, the exact nature of the child's difficulties is determined. Then a structured, sequential approach is used to overcome these difficulties. Material is organised logically and reflects the nature of the English language. Many educators advocate a multi-sensory approach, involving all of the child's senses to reinforce learning, such as listening to the way a word sounds, seeing the way a letter or word looks, and feeling the movement of hand or mouth muscles in producing a spoken or written letter, word or sound.

CASE STUDY

Natalie

Natalie is 7 and attends a mainstream primary school. Although she is a bright and intelligent child, with particularly advanced skills in drawing, it has become increasingly obvious that she is having difficulty in reading, writing and spelling. Natalie's behaviour in class is deteriorating to such an extent that she is stopping other children working. She has become the class clown and her teacher is finding it difficult to keep her 'on task'.

1 Explain why Natalie's difficulty in reading has resulted in a deterioration in her behaviour.

2 Suggest ways of helping Natalie improve her behaviour.

3 The class teacher has initiated the identification and assessment procedure under the 1994 Code of Practice. Describe what will happen next. (You will have to research this. The document is available from the DfEE. If you are attached to a school, the Special Educational Needs Co-ordinator should be able to help you.)

Vision and dyslexia

Children with dyslexia need to have their eyes tested because certain conditions have been found to be associated with dyslexia, although the eye problems are not the cause of the difficulties with reading.

✔ PROGRESS CHECK

1 In your own words, describe the difficulties a child with dyslexia may have.

2 What percentage of children have dyslexia?

3 List three ways that a child-care practitioner can help a pre-school child who may have dyslexia.

4 How may dyslexia affect a child's emotional and social development?

5 Describe three ways a child with dyslexia can be helped in school.

KEY TERMS

You need to know the meaning of the following words and phrases. Go back through the chapter to make sure you understand them:

autism
Asperger syndrome
developmental verbal dyspraxia
dysfluent speech
dyslexia
meconium
metaphor
over-learning
stammering
statutory provision
voluntary provision

FURTHER READING

Dare, A. and O'Donovan, M. (1997) *Good Practice in Caring for Children with Special Needs*, Stanley Thornes
This is an excellent book, suitable for everyone caring for children. The book gives up-to-date information about children with special needs and also looks at some of the underlying principles of their care.
Law, J. (ed.) (1992) *The Early Identification of Language Impairment in Children*, Chapman & Hall
This book is more specialised and is recommended for individuals working in this field, or for students on level four courses.

Glossary

1994 Code of Practice a government document which sets out the principles and procedures for the identification, assessment and review of children with special educational needs in schools

accent the way that words are pronounced in a particular region or country

American Sign Language (ASL) the standard sign language used by the deaf community in North America

articulate to produce speech sounds in the mouth and throat

Asperger syndrome a condition similar to autism where an individual has difficulty communicating and relating to others, but who has appropriate language skills and does not have learning difficulties

auditory-oral method children are trained to use any hearing they have, to lipread and to speak

autism a disability that prevents individuals understanding the world around them through their senses, with associated problems in communication, social relationships and behaviour

auxiliary verb a verb which is used with another verb in a sentence and which shows grammatical functions such as time or person, for example, *she is working* or *they have finished*

babbling repeated sounds produced by babies when they are about 6 months old, consisting of **vowel–consonant** combinations

balanced bilingual a person who can listen, speak, read and write with equal proficiency in two languages

bilingual literally, two languages – in everyday use, a bilingual person is someone who speaks two langues; it refers to people who have access to a second **linguistic code**, but do not necessarily have full skills of listening, reading, speaking and writing in either language; see **balanced bilingual**

Blissymbols a universal language of pictographic symbols which is used by people with reading and writing disabilities

Braille a touch-based reading and writing system used by people who are blind

British Sign Language (BSL) the sign language used by the deaf community in the UK

clause a group of words that form a grammatical unit and contain a subject and a verb; see also **embedded clause**

closed question a question that only requires a one-word answer, for instance *Do you like sweets?*, to which the answer can be either *yes* or *no*; see also **open question**

cochlear implant an implant which replaces the inner ear and electronically stimulates the nerve of hearing

cognitive a term used loosely to refer to a range of abstract skills – thinking, reasoning, understanding, problem-solving, etc.

composition the expression of ideas in writing

conductive hearing loss deafness caused by the impaired passage of sound waves in the ear

consonant a speech sound where the breath is partially obstructed by the tongue or lips. The sounds correspond to the letters $b, c, d, f, g, h, j, k, l, m, n, p, q, r, s, t, v, w, x, y, z$

contentives the essential words in speech that carry the content of a communication

contextual understanding the choice of words, or the body language used, may depend on the situation

cooing sounds produced by babies at around 6 weeks of age, usually indicating pleasure, consisting of repeated vowel sounds mixed with laughing

cued speech a system of eight hand-shapes made in four locations near the face to assist children who are deaf (or adults) in lipreading

cultural norms the rules or standards of behaviour in a particular group which specify what is appropriate or inappropriate behaviour

cultural understanding the language or culture of the speaker or listener may influence what is said or heard

cursive script writing where the individual letters in each word are joined to each other

data the facts gathered from studies; note that data are plural – *data are...*

deaf culture the customs, history and way of life of people who are deaf

developmental verbal dyspraxia (DVD) a condition where a child has difficulties in producing speech sounds and in putting these sounds together in the correct sequence to form words

developmental writing the idea that children actively explore and experiment with writing

dialect a form of language spoken in a particular region or by members of a particular group or class of people, distinguished by the vocabulary (words used), **grammar**, pronunciation (**accent**) and use of **idiom**; dialects are also referred to as speech varieties

divergent thinking being able to think in different ways about something

dysfluent speech speech that is not smooth and continuous, often heard in young children

dyslexia a disorder where children have difficulties in learning to read and write, despite conventional instruction, adequate intelligence and adequate home environment

egocentric in Piaget's terms, being unable to take the point of view of another

embedded clause a **clause** that is put within a sentence. For instance, *that he got married* in the sentence *The news, that he got married, surprised his friends.*

emergent literacy the beginning stages of reading and writing where the child develops an awareness of printed material without formal teaching

emergent writing the reading and writing behaviours of young children before they develop into conventional literacy

empiricist a philosophical approach that holds the view that all knowledge comes from experience

environmental print the printed words that are found in the world around us, other than books and newspapers, for instance street names and shop signs

ethnolinguistic group a small (minority) group within a community or country which has its own language and culture

expressive language the ability to communicate verbally

fluent handwriting handwriting that the writer finds comfortable to produce. There is a comfortable grip of the pen, the body is relaxed and the letters are formed correctly

grammar the system of rules that are applied when using language

grammatical markers or inflections the sounds added to a sentence to make the meaning more precise

heritage language the language which has been passed on from generation to generation in the cultural group to which the child belongs; usually spoken at home by a child's parents; also known as **home language**; the preferred term to **mother tongue**

historical linguist a **linguist** who studies language change and language relationships

holophrase a single word, often accompanied by gesture or change in intonation, that carries the meaning of a sentence

home language another term for **heritage language**; preferred to **mother tongue**

hypothesis a theory about something that is not yet proved but which serves as a basis for further research

idiom an expression whose meaning cannot be worked out from its separate parts, for example, *I have washed my hands of the matter* meaning I have no intention of having anything more to do with the matter

infant print the first style of writing taught to children – letters are printed in the lower case with capitals for the beginning of sentences and names

inferior pincer grip or grasp a grip used by babies when they pick up small objects between their thumb and index finger; the tip of the index finger is not used

innate something which exists or has the potential to exist at birth by virtue of genetic factors

institutional disregard when it is accepted in public institutions, e.g. schools, within a country or community that the needs of a group of people and/or their language are not important enough to be considered

internalise the acceptance of values, beliefs, attitudes and standards as one's own

interpersonal skills the skill of interacting in a reciprocal way between two people

intonation the patterns or tunes of speech produced by lowering and raising the voice when speaking

intuitive understanding having a feeling or sense that things are a certain way without being told

jargon the use of non-word sounds in the older baby

language pragmatics the way language is used

legible easy to read

linguist someone who studies the way language began and developed during the course of human history; also studies the structure of language; see also **historical linguist, linguistic code, linguistics, psycholinguist**

linguistic code a term used instead of the word *language* to describe a language being used in a community

linguistics the scientific study of language; see also **linguist; historical linguist, linguistic code, psycholinguist**

lipreading identifying what a speaker is saying by studying the movements of the lips and face muscles

longitudinal studies studies carried out over an extended period of time

Makaton a basic signing system using signs borrowed from British Sign Language, used by people who have severe learning difficulties

mark-making the act of making marks which involves 'creativity, communication and some degree of permanence' (Marion Whitehead)

meconium the first stool a baby passes after birth. If passed before birth it may indicate that the baby is in distress

metalinguistic skills being able to think about what language is for and how it is used

metaphor a figure of speech where something is described by stating another thing. For instance, *his words stabbed at her heart*

monolingual a person who knows and uses only one language

monologue a long speech by one person

monosyllabic words words which contain only one syllable, such as *cat;* see also **polysyllabic words**

mother tongue the first language which is acquired at home; the terms **heritage language** or **home language** are now more widely used

narrative form the style of writing used to tell a story; see also **non-narrative form**

native speaker a speaker of a language acquired in early childhood because it is spoken in the family and it is the language of the country where the person lives

non-narrative form the style of writing used to write reports, instructions, etc.; see also **narrative form**

non-verbal communication any action or gesture or use of the body

179

which communicates information without making use of speech; also referred to as body language

norms   characteristic behaviours of a group

noun   a **word** used to denote a person, place or thing, for example, *dog*, *daddy*, *park*

onomatopoeia   the use of words which imitate the thing named, e.g. cuckoo, bang, snap

open question   a question that encourages a response of more than one word, for instance *What did you do yesterday?*; see also **closed question**

oral method   a way of teaching language to children who are deaf through lipreading and shaping of speech

over-learning   the use of constant repetition and practice of a skill such as letter formation

palmar grasp   the grasp used by young babies when an object is picked up by the palm, with the fingers curling around the object. There is little control of the finger muscles

paralanguage   the many ways in which a **word** can be said, including the use of gestures, eye movements, tone of voice, used to add emphasis and meaning to what is said

paraphrase   using other words in an attempt to make the meaning of what has been said easier to understand

passive   where the object of a sentence becomes the subject, for instance, the sentence *The wind damaged the fence* becomes *The fence **was damaged by** the wind* in the passive form

phonemes   the basic sounds of any human language. Different languages are composed of different numbers and combinations of phonemes

phonics   the sound of letters and letter combinations

phonology   the study of the sound units of a language and their relationship to each other

pincer grip or grasp   a grasp involving the tip of the thumb and first finger, used to pick up small objects

pitch   how high or low speech sounds are, relative to each other, as perceived by the listener

polysyllabic words   words that contain more than one syllable; see also **monosyllabic words**

predisposition   factors in our genetic make-up that increase the likelihood of us being able to display a particular characteristic

preferred hand   the hand that we prefer to write with

pre-linguistic stage of language development   in the baby's first year of life, when the baby develops sounds and gestures, before the emergence of her first words

profoundly deaf   total deafness, as opposed to partial deafness

programme music   music which is set to a story – sounds and instruments are used to depict features of the story

proxemes   the physical distance between people when they are talking to each other, as well as their posture and whether or not there is physical contact during their conversation

psycholinguist   someone who studies the mental processes that are used in producing and understanding language and also how humans learn language

reading   understanding the meaning of written or printed words or symbols, or speaking such words aloud

receptive language   the ability to understand the meaning of words

receptive system   a system which helps people who are deaf to know the exact sound intended

reduplicated monosyllable   the repetition of a sound, for example, *mama*

reformulated   where some of the words used may be different, or in slightly different order, but the message given is the same

reinforcer   anything that strengthens or supports an action so that that action is repeated

representations   internalised thoughts that help us think about and recall things and people in their absence

semantics   meanings of language

sensori-motor period in Piagetian theory, the stage of cognitive functioning between birth and 18 months

sensori-neural hearing loss deafness caused by damage to the sensory cells of the inner ear, or to the nervous system associated with hearing

sign language the manual and gestural system of communication used by people who are deaf; the sign languages used in different countries are languages in their own right, and not manual means of communicating the spoken languages of those countries; see **American Sign Language**, **British Sign Language**

sound discrimination the ability to hear the difference between sounds

speech variety another term for **dialect**

stage one grammar the stage in a child's language development when she or he begins to use short, simple sentences (roughly from 18–30 months)

stage two grammar the stage of language development when a child progresses from using simple, short sentences to using sentences that are longer and more complicated (roughly from 30 months–3 years)

stammering an abnormal speech pattern where there are hesitations and repetitions that break the flow of speech

Standard English the English which has the highest status in the English-speaking world and which is based on the speech and writing of educated speakers

statutory provision provision (services) which has to be provided by law

stereotypes over-generalisations about a group or class of people usually based on biased or inaccurate beliefs

subjective dependent on an individual's way of thinking

symbol anything that represents, or indicates, something else, for instance a doll that represents a baby, a letter representing a sound, a number that represents a quantity

syntax grammar – the way that words go together (word order) to form meaningful phrases and sentences

telegraphic speech the shortened, simple form of speech used by toddlers in which only the essential words are used

tokenistic something which is available as a minimum concession to satisfy racial demands; having diverse cultural resources available because it seems the right thing to do but not using them

transcription the secretarial aspects of writing such as spelling, punctuation and handwriting

tripod grasp or grip a grip that is used to pick up an object between the thumb and first two fingers

utterance producing spoken language, either words or sentences

variable any feature of the testing or observation that is apt to vary, for example the amount of light in a room or the words used by the researcher to ask a question

verb an action word, for example, *go, see, eat*

voluntary provision provision (services) that meets a need within the community but which does not have to be provided by law

vowel a speech sound made with the mouth open (i.e. not involving the lips or tongue) that corresponds to the letters *a, e, i, o, u*

word a sound that is used as a symbol in a language community to refer to something specific

Resources

For children who stammer

The British Stammering Association
15 Old Ford Road
London
E2 9PJ
Tel: 0181 983 1003
Helpline: 0845 603 2001

I CAN
The National Educational Charity for
Children with Speech and Language Disorders
Barbican
Citygate
London
EC1Y 8NA

For children with developmental verbal dyspraxia

AFASIC – Overcoming Speech Impairments
347 Central Markets
Smithfield
London
EC1A 9NH
Tel: 0171 236 3632

For children who are autistic

The National Autistic Society
393 City Road
London
EC1V 1NE
Tel: 0171 833 2299

For children who are dyslexic

The British Dyslexia Association
98 London Road
Reading
RG1 5AU
Tel: (helpline) 0118 9668271
(administration) 0118 9662677

The Dyslexia Institute
133 Gresham Road
Staines
Middlesex
TW18 2AJ
Tel: 01784 463851

For children who are deaf

The British Deaf Association
1–3 Worship Street
London
EC2 2AB
Tel: 0171 588 3520 (voice)
0171 588 3529 (minicom)

The Royal National Institute for the Deaf (RNID)
19–23 Featherstone Street
London
EC1Y 8SL
Tel: 0171 296 800 (voice)
0171 383 3154 (minicom)

The National Deaf Children's Society
15 Dufferin Street
London
EC1Y 8SL

Reading resources

Storysacks
Storysacks starter information pack:
Neil Griffiths 01793 421168

Letterbox library
Leroy House
Essex Road
London N1
Tel: 0171 226 1633

A book distributor that provides material that is non-racist and non-sexist. Book reviews and newsletters are also available.

Community Insight
The Pembroke Centre
Cheney Manor
Swindon
SN2 2PQ
Tel: 01793 512612

A specialist bookseller in the field of child-care and education. They have a wide range of books for children

The London Language and Literacy Unit
Southwark College
Southampton Way
London
SE5 7EW
Tel: 0171 639 9512

A unit that works in the areas of basic skills, family literacy and numeracy, ESOL, Caribbean languages and literature, language and learning support.

Book Trust
Book House
45 East Hill
London SW18 2QZ
Tel: 0181 516 2977

A charitable organisation that supplies lists of books suitable for this age range.

The Federation of Children's Book Groups
9 Westroyd
Pudsey
West Yorkshire
Tel: 0113 257 9950

An organisation that can provide book lists and advice.

Government departments

Qualifications and Curriculum Authority (QCA)
Newcombe House
45 Notting Hill Gate
London
W11 3JB

QCA Publications
PO Box 235
Hayes
Middlesex
UB3 1HF
Tel: 0181 867 3333

Department for Education and Employment (DfEE)
DfEE Publications
PO Box 5050
Sudbury
Suffolk
CO10 6ZQ

Index

Accents 4, 66, 143, 144
American Sign Language
    (ASL) 152
Anecdotal records 19
Animal studies 3, 23, 24, 32, 64, 65
Art 12
    Good Practice 13
Articulation 4, 67
Asperger syndrome 168
Assessment 94
Audio recordings 21
Auditory-oral method 155
Autism 168–70
Auxiliary verb 47

Babbling 39
Baby talk register 30
Baseline assessment 95, 96, 118
Behaviourist 26
    arguments in favour of 27
    arguments against 27
    theories of language
      development 26
Bilingualism
    advantages of 130, 133, 134
    attitudes to 127–30
    balanced bilingual 126
    bilingualism and education
      129, 135–8
    bilingualism and intelligence
      132–4
    current situation 130
    deaf bilingualism 154–6
    Definition 125, 127
    dominant bilingual 126
    effects of early research 129,
      130
    Good Practice 138, 140
    helping young children 138, 139
    historical perspective 128–30
    immersion programmes 136,
      137
    institutional disregard 128
    keeping records and assessment
      140, 141
    learning a second language 138,
      139
    maintenance and enrichment
      137

myths about bilingualism, 131
    passive bilingual 126
    transitional bilingual 126, 136
    simultaneous bilingual 127
Biological theory 29
Blissymbols 152
Body Language 8, 11,
    cultural differences 10
    in children 11
    kinesics 9
Books
    choosing 86
    sharing with children 87, 88
Book area 86
Bottom-up model *see* Reading
Boys and reading 99
Boys and writing 115
Braille 152
British Sign Language (BSL) 152
Brunner, Jerome 31

Checklist 94
Chomsky, Noam 29, 30, 33
Cochlear implant 151
Computers 123, 124
Communication
    body language 8–11
    Definition 5
    intuitive understanding 5
    non-verbal 6
    shared meaning 5, 6
    through art, music, drama and
      dance 5, 12–16
    with young children 6
Composition 103
Conductive hearing loss 147
Consonant 39
Contentives 45
Contextual understanding 59
Cooing 37
Cross-cultural studies 25
Cross-sectional studies 24
Crying 37
Cued Speech 152, 154
Cultural tools 6
Cultural understanding 59
Culture
    differences in language 10
    internalisation of 130

transmission through language
    6, 130
Cursive script 119

Dance 16
Deaf education
    history of 156
    oralist tradition 154, 155
    20th century 157
Deaf culture 154
Deafness
    auditory brainstem evaluation
      151
    British Sign Language (BSL)
      152
    cochlear implant 151
    conductive deafness 147
    deaf bilingualism 154–6
    deaf culture 154
    Good Practice 150
    history of deaf education 156
    incidence 147
    indications of hearing
      impairments 149
    manual communication 152
    oralist tradition 154, 155
    otoacoustic emissions 151
    sensori-neural deafness 147,
      148
    sign languages 146, 152
    treatments and interventions
      151
    types of hearing assessment
      150
Developmental Verbal Dyspraxia
    (DVD) 163, 164
Developmental writing 106
Dialects 66, 143, 144
Diaries 19
Displays 93
Divergent thinking 134
Drama 15
DVD *see* Developmental Verbal
    Dyspraxia
Dual texts 142
Dysfluent speech 161
Dyslexia 172
    causes of 173
    Definition 172

Good Practice 173–4
identification of children 172, 173
incidence 172
treatments and interventions 175
use of computers 174

Echolalia 39
Expressive language 41
Egocentric 34
Emergent literacy 83
Emergent writing 83
Empiricist 26
Environmental print 80
Ethnolinguistic group 128–9
Eye contact 9

Feral children 32, 65

Gaelscoileanna 136
Gestures 40
Grammar
Definition 19
rules of early sentences 45
Grammatical markers 44, 47

Hand-eye co-ordination 104, 105
Handwriting 118–22
Historical linguist 65
Heritage language 129
Holophrase 44

Idiom 4
Infant print 119
Inferior pincer grip 105
Inflection 44
Imaginative play area 92, 116
Innate
Definition 29
Innate theories
arguments in favour of 29
arguments against 29
Interactive model *see* Reading
Interpersonal skills 60
Intonation 4
Intuitive understanding 6

Jargon 42

Kinesics 9
Key worker system 38

Language
in animals 3, 24, 64
body language 8
Definition 1, 3
development, summary of 53–5
expressive 41
first word 41
first sentences 44

Good Practice 41, 42, 43, 46, 48, 50
language pragmatics 51
older child 50
one word stage 41
origin of 2
over-3s 48, 49
over-regularisation 47
pre-linguistic stage 37
receptive 41
rules of 4
and self-control 52
and thought 33, 34
signed languages 152
stage one grammar 44
stage two grammar 46
theoretical approaches to language development 26
Language Acquisition Device (LAD) 29
Language Acquisition Support System (LASS) 31
Linguists 2
Linguistic code 126
Lipreading 154
Listening
Definition 57
different ways of listening 60–3
Early Years Curriculum 56
Good Practice 63
listening effectively 62, 63
listening skills 58
listening in schools and nurseries 69–73
value of 63, 64
with young children 87–73
Listening area 86
Literacy 83–93
Literacy Hour 96, 97, 118
Longitudinal study 19, 24

Makaton 152, 165–7
Manual communication 152
Mark making 81, 106
Metalinguistic 134
Metaphor 168
Methodology 19
Monolingual 126
Monologue 34
Motherese 30
Mother tongue 129
Multilingualism *see* Bilingualism
Music 13
Good Practice 14

Narrative form 118
Natavist theory 29
National Curriculum 96, 118
National Literacy Hour 96

Native speaker 127
Nature 30
Non-verbal (*see also* Communication and Body language) 6, 11, 168
Norm
Definition 25
Nurture 30

Observations 20, 94
Onomatopoeic words 65
Oral method 154, 155

Palmar grasp 105
Paralanguage 10
Parent/carer 97, 98
Phonology 4
Piaget 33
Pincer grip 105
Pitch 4
Pivot words 45
Planning 94
Poetry 92
Predisposition 29
Preferred hand 105
Pre-linguistic stage 37
Print 83
Profoundly deaf (see also Deafness) 147
Programme music 7
Phonemes 4
Phonology 4
Proxeme 9
Psycholinguists 3

Questions 47, 49

Reading 74–100
alphabetical method 78
as a skill 85
assessment 94
bottom-up model 77
boys and 99
Definition 74
developing reading in 3–5-year-olds 83–94
developing reading in 5–7-year-olds 95–9
early predictions of success 85
foundations for learning in under threes 80–2
government guidelines 95–7
interactive approach 77, 79
phonic method 78
real books method 79
sentence method 79
theoretical approaches 76–9
top-down model 77
word method 78
Receptive language 4
Receptive system 154

Reduplicated monosyllable   39
Reinforcer   26
Representations   81
Research   23
   animal studies   3, 23
   cross-cultural studies   25
   cross-sectional studies   24
   laboratory studies   25
   longitudinal studies   24
Rhymes   92
Role model   7
Role play   15, 92, 116

Scribble   107
Sapir-Whorf hypothesis   34
Sentences 44–6
Sensori-motor period   33
Sensori-neural hearing loss   147
Semantics   4
Sign languages   146, 153
Skinner, B. F.   26
Social interactionist approach to
   language development   3
Sound
   awareness of   37
   differences between animals and
     humans   64, 65
   discrimination   37
   Standard English   66
Speaking   64–7
   with young children   67–73
   Good Practice with young children
     71

Speech
   development   32, 64, 65
   different uses of   51, 65

Spelling   122
Stage one grammar   44
Stammering   159, 160, 161
Standard English   66
Stories
   props   90
   sequencing   91
   story time   89
   story sacks   91
   telling stories   90
   value of   88
Stuttering *see* Stammering
Symbols   81
Syntax   4

Telegraphic speech   45
Tone   9
Theories   18
   behaviourist   26–8
   innate   29
   learning   26
   social interactionist   31, 32
Top-down model *see* Reading
Transcription   103
Tripod grasp   105
Turn-taking   31

Universal grammars   29
Utterance   31

Variable
   Definition   24
Verbal Dyspraxia *see*
   Developmental Verbal
   Dyspraxia
Video recordings   22
Vocabulary   4, 42

Vocal Paralanguage *see* Paralanguage
Vowel   37
Vygotsky, Lev   33, 34

Writing
   boys and writing   115
   comparison of oral and written
     language   102
   composition   103
   computers and writing   103
   cursive script   119
   Definition   101, 102
   developmental approach   113
   developmental writing skills, 3–5
     years   106–17
   emergent writing   109
   Good Practice   122
   handwriting style   118,   119
   infant print   119
   left-handed writers   119
   mark-making   106
   preferred hand   105
   role of the adult   113, 114,
     121
   scribble   107
   traditional approach   112
   transcription   103
   uses of writing   102, 103
   what children need to learn
     103
   writing area   114
   writing skills, 5–7-year-olds
     118
Word
   Definition   3
   word meaning   32